GM INTERCITY COACHES 1944-1980

PHOTO ARCHIVE

Brian Grams & Andrew Gold

Iconografix
Photo Archive Series

Iconografix
PO Box 446
Hudson, Wisconsin 54016 USA

Library of Congress Control Number: 2003103534

ISBN 1-58388-099-2

03 04 05 06 07 08 09 5 4 3 2 1

Printed in China

Cover and book design by Dan Perry

Copyediting by Suzie Helberg

COVER PHOTO: Boise-Winnemucca Stages is based in Boise, Idaho. Shown is 1968 PD-4903-152, their fleet No. 143. The photo was taken at Pontiac, Michigan.

DEDICATION

I dedicate this book to my wife Rena and to my kids, Julia, Mason, Callan and Kimberley for without their patience and understanding I could not have taken the time to gather the photos and information shared here. Just as this book was being finished my father, Walter August Grams (Wally), passed away at 83 years of age. Dad drove for Greyhound Canada from the time that he returned from Europe where he served during WWII with the Royal Canadian Air Force until his retirement in 1984. He drove many of the coaches shown in this book and I thank him for his stories and his memories. *Brian W. Grams*

I would like to thank my family for their years of support (and tolerance) for my interest in this hobby. The work of other enthusiasts whose material appears in this book is also greatly appreciated. *Andrew A. Gold*

ACKNOWLEDGMENTS

The photographs in this book are from many sources. These books are an excellent way for historians and enthusiasts to share the wealth of material that they have. We gratefully acknowledge the generosity and assistance of all contributors and especially thank the following:

Donald M. Bain, Kishorn Publications, Calgary, Alberta
Donald Coffin, Bus Industry Historian, Hawley, Pennsylvania
Dave Dyck, Director Environmental Affairs, Greyhound Canada Transportation Corp., Calgary, Alberta
Tom Jones, Librarian, Motor Bus Society, Clark, New Jersey
Loring M. Lawrence, Secretary, Bus History Association, Manchester, New Hampshire
Paul Leger, Bus History Association, Halifax, Nova Scotia
William and Adelene Luke, Retired, Spokane, Washington
Peter Newgard, President, Canadian Transit Heritage Foundation, Ottawa, Ontario
Charles R. Sullivan, President, Motor Bus Society, Paramus, New Jersey

AUTHORS' NOTE: This book is a continuation of the work *Yellow Coach Buses 1923-1943 Photo Archive* by William A. Luke. When we undertook to prepare this work we had photos of all the highway or "parlor" coaches that had been built under the General Motors nameplate. As we gathered these photos we kept in mind a comment made in a book review about one of Brian's earlier works. The opinion of this reviewer was that most of the photos were sterile or "roster" shots with little background or scenery. We sent out requests to various people and history organizations for photos of the buses at work in various settings. We were overwhelmed by the response. We received so many photos that we really ended up compiling photos from others and writing about these. We hope the reader is pleased with the captions that talk about the setting and the bus company as well as the coach.

We would like to mention two excellent organizations that were most helpful with this book and continue to be rich resources for those interested in the bus industry. Both are most worthy of your support.

Motor Bus Society Inc.
PO Box 251
Paramus, New Jersey 07653
motorbussociety@yahoo.com

Bus History Association
11 Arlington Avenue
Halifax, Nova Scotia B3N 1Z7

You are encouraged to support these people and to share material with others.

INTRODUCTION

GM History and Models Built

The General Motors Truck & Coach Division traces its roots back to April 17, 1923 when the Yellow Coach Manufacturing Company was established by John D. Hertz. In 1915, Hertz and an associate started the Yellow Cab Company of Chicago and founded the Yellow Cab Manufacturing Company to build taxicabs for their own company as well as for sale to others.

In 1922, Hertz purchased The Lake Shore Motor Bus Company, which was a holding company for The Chicago Motor Coach Co. Through this purchase, the American Motor Bus Company (a subsidiary of Chicago Motor Coach) became part of Yellow.

On April 17, 1923 the Yellow Coach Manufacturing Company was formed as a subsidiary of the Yellow Cab Company and a new factory was opened in Chicago in August 1923. Alfred Sloan, president of General Motors Corporation, soon proposed a merger so that GM would be involved in bus building. In this merger, GM sold the General Motors Truck Corporation to Yellow in exchange for a controlling interest in the company that would be formed to combine the two businesses. In August 1925, Yellow Truck & Coach Manufacturing was established. This was the company that purchased the GM Truck Division. General Motors, in turn, purchased all the common shares of Yellow Truck & Coach, which amounted to about 57 percent of the total capital investment of the company.

The GM Truck Corporation had been formed by the acquisition of the Reliance Motor Truck Company of Owosso and the Rapid Motor Vehicle Company of Pontiac, Michigan. In the spring of 1926, it was decided to combine all bus and truck building at a new plant to be built in Pontiac. A 1,250,000 square-foot building was built on a 160-acre site that General Motors had acquired in 1926 for future expansion. The first truck came out of this plant on January 5, 1928, and bus and taxi production was also moved out of Chicago into Pontiac in 1928.

During 1943, General Motors purchased the minority interest in Yellow Truck & Coach Manufacturing Co., and effective October 1, 1943, Yellow became a division of GM under the name General Motors Truck & Coach Division. It is the coaches of this latter company that are discussed in this book.

The first GM buses were built in 1943 when the War Production Board (WPB) authorized production of 1,340 transit buses. The first highway GMs were built in 1944 when 700 parlor cars were allowed by the WPB.

Between August, 1923 and May, 1987 approximately 128,000 buses were built by Yellow/GM plus about another 12,000 built in Canada by the Diesel Division of GM of Canada, Ltd. The buses built in Canada were transit types. All the buses shown in this book were built in Pontiac, Michigan including those for delivery in Canada.

In the late 1940s, Greyhound US, through its wholly owned subsidiary Western Canadian Greyhound Lines, had purchased an interest in a small Canadian bus builder called Motor Coach Industries (MCI). This purchase was completed ten years later and steps were then taken to have MCI develop and build a coach suitable for use by Greyhound US as well as Greyhound in Canada. Early steps in this evolution included the MC-1 with a 4-71 General Motors diesel motor and air ride but with no lavatory or air conditioning. This model would have been a major step backwards for Greyhound US, which had been running coaches equipped with diesels, air ride and rest rooms for many years. MCI moved on to the MC-2 and the MC-3, both of which had the 6V-71 diesel and offered both rest rooms and air conditioning. These were still underpowered compared with the PD-4501 and the PD-4106, which were using the 8V-71 by this time. The next step for MCI was the MC-4 using the 8V-71 and it was almost what GH US was looking for. Improvements to this coach resulted in the building of the MC-5, which is what GH US bought in quantity. In 1963, MCI opened a finishing plant in Pembina, North Dakota, which completed the coach "shells" built in Winnipeg, Manitoba, just across the border.

MCI could still not build enough coaches for Greyhound's needs so there was an overlap of purchases with GH buying GMs until MCI could build MC-5s in quantity.

Other operators followed Greyhound's lead and started to buy the MCI buses and GM finally abandoned the parlor car line in 1980. The labor costs and materials added up to more than the coach could be sold for. Also, by 1980 the basic parlor coach design was almost 30 years old and the high level design was 14 years old. GM was faced with the prospect of a major research and development cost in order to compete with MCI and Eagle.

The following chart outlines the basic GM models. We have included the Yellow models 719 and 743 since these were the first real "coaches". Often called "Super Coaches", the 719/743 were the first rear engined coaches with the entrance door in front of the steering axle and space for luggage and freight in sealed bays or tanks underneath the passenger compartment.

The Super Coaches were the first highway coaches to use the transverse rear engine and angle drive and the last of them had diesel engines. General Motors had acquired patents to the "V" drive when it hired Dwight Austin who had developed it for the defunct Pickwick Corporation's bus manufacturing plant in California. The V-drive arrangement is where the engine is mounted side to side at the rear of the coach and the power is transmitted to the rear axle by way of an angle drive. The T-drive is where the engine is mounted straight in with power transmitted straight to the drive axle.

Model	Wheel Base (inches)	Engine	Drive	Quantity Built	Dates Built	Notes
719	245	707 gas	v-drive	325	1936	built by Yellow Coach
743	245	707, 6-71	v-drive	1256	1937-1939	built by Yellow Coach
PGA-3702	239	477gas	t-drive	600	1944-1945	Pontiac Motor Division
PDA-3702	239	4-71	t-drive	600	1945	Pontiac Motor Division
PD-3302	212	4-71	t-drive	100	1945	Pontiac Motor Division
PD-2903	218	4-71	t-drive	400	1946-1949	
PG-2904	218	426 gas	t-drive	200	1946-1949	
PDA-3703	239	4-71	t-drive	750	1947-1949	
PD-3751	264	6-71	v-drive	1643	1947-1948	"Silversides"
PD-4151	264	6-71	v-drive	357	1948	"Silversides"
PDA-4101	247	6-71	v-drive	335	1948-1950	
PDA-3704	239	4-71	t-drive	100	1950	
PD-4102	247	6-71	v-drive	115	1950-1951	
PGA-3301	242	503 gas	t-drive	840	1951	U.S. Army specifications
PD-4103	247	6-71	v-drive	1501	1951-1952	
PD-4104	261	6-71	v-drive	5065	1953-1960	first parlor air ride
PD-4501	259.5	2x 4-71	t-drive	1001	1954-1956	"Scenicruiser"
PD-4901	259.5	2x 4-71	t-drive	1	1954	"Golden Chariot"
PD-4106	261	8V-71	v-drive	3227	1964-1965	
PD-4107	261	8V-71	v-drive	1267	1966-1969	first parlor auto
PD-4108	261	8V-71	v-drive	65	1970-1971	
P8M-4108A	261	8V-71	v-drive	232	1972-1978	
PD-4903	318.5	8V-71	v-drive	401	1968-1969	
PD-4905	318.5	8V-71	v-drive	330	1970-1971	
P8M-4905A	318.5	8V-71	v-drive	2002	1972-1978	
H8H-649	318.5	8V-71	v-drive	233	1979-1980	

MODEL NAMES

This is the first generation used by GM from 1944 to 1972.

P – parlor or highway coach.

D – diesel engine. **G** – gasoline engine.

A – used if model name had been used by Yellow prior to the change to GM (PG-3301 vs. PG**A**-3301 which were different buses).

Next two numbers - nominal seating capacity (without rest room).

Last two numbers - actual model number (PD-4104 often called 04s).

The second generation had minor changes and was used from 1972 to 1979.

8 – the number 8 replaced **D** for diesel and it showed the coach utilized the 8V-71 diesel engine. This would have allowed for the then new 6V-92 or 8V-92 motors, which were never used in the parlor cars.

M – this letter was added to indicate the coach had a manual gearbox with the letter **H** here designating an automatic (or hydraulic) transmission. In practice most, if not all, of the highway coaches built with the automatic were still designated P8M- for some reason.

A - air conditioned. This last letter was added in the late sixties to designate transit coaches with air conditioning. Even though all the highway coaches built at this time were air conditioned, this **A** was added to the parlor models as well. (e.g. P8M-4108**A**).

If there is a second group of digits after the model, then this is the "serial number". For example: PD-4104 is the basic model and PD-4104-2255 is the serial number.

The third generation was used from 1979 to the end of parlor car production in 1980.

H8H-649: **H** is for Highway; **8** designates a 40-foot coach (8x5-foot sections); the second **H** is for the 8V-71 engine (engine had production code "H"); **6** = 96-inch width; **49** = nominal passenger rating.

The unbuilt 35-foot coach would have been the H7H-641.

GENERAL MOTORS TWO-STROKE DIESEL ENGINES

Perhaps the true "genius", if you will, of the Yellow and GM coaches was the General Motors two-stroke diesel engine. This basic motor was developed in the 1930s and first installed in transit buses in 1937 and in the last of the Model 743 parlor coaches built in 1939. The two-stroke diesel, as opposed to the four stroke, fires on every down stroke, which results in more power being produced by a smaller displacement engine. This increase was not quite two-to-one but a 200-cubic-inch, two-stroke engine, will produce almost as much horsepower and torque as a 400-cubic-inch, four-stroke engine.

GM produced "families" of engines, which shared many parts. The most common diesel for the coach industry was the -71 series. This meant that each cylinder displaced 71 cubic inches. Different engines were built using different numbers of cylinders. The 4-71, 6-71, 6V-71 and 8V-71 were common coach engines. The 4-71 was an inline four, the 6-71 an inline six, and the other two were built in the "V" configuration. Since there are no intake or exhaust strokes with a two-stroke engine all these engines are supercharged. Air pressure from the supercharger forces the burned exhaust gases from the cylinder when the exhaust valves open and also provides the fresh air needed for the next power stroke.

Pacific Greyhound No. 325 was the first production Yellow Model 719 and the first of 50 to go to Pacific Greyhound. It has been stopped in Kansas City, Missouri for some publicity photos. The setting is Lake of the Woods – Swope Park in 1936. Although never built under the GM nameplate the 719 and is shown here as it and the 743 were the first real highway "coaches".

The 719 and 743 were models built before the takeover of Yellow by GM and were the first true coaches with the engine at the rear, the entrance door in front of the steering axle and the luggage underneath the passengers. This photo shows Pacific Greyhound Lines No. 329 (a Model 719) repainted in the "Battle of Britain" paint scheme.

Ohio Greyhound Lines No. 775 was a Model 743 configured as a 23-passenger club coach with two-and-one seating, assigned to run from Detroit to Florida. Although the coach is equipped with air conditioning, as shown by the air intake grille above the rear wheels, the windows could still be opened when needed. Both the driver's window and the entrance door window could also be rolled down for extra ventilation. The 719/743 introduced the Dwight Austin angle drive to the Yellow highway coaches and the last 34 Model 743s were the first highway coaches to use the newly developed two-stroke General Motors diesel. This was the 6-71 which was coupled to a four-speed manual transmission.

Ohio Greyhound No. 766 is shown leaving the Toledo depot bound for Cincinnati at 1:11 on a fine summer's afternoon. It is a non-air conditioned 743 and the passengers have opened some of the windows to get a bit of fresh air.

The PGA-3702 (gas engine) used the 477-cubic-inch, in-line, six-cylinder gas engine and the PDA-3702 used the 4-71 General Motors two-stroke diesel engine. Both engines were mounted straight in. Most of the PGAs were later re-powered with the 4-71 diesel when that engine became available in quantity following World War II. Boston & Maine Transportation Company No. 770 is a PDA-3702.

When coach production was allowed to resume in 1944, the GM bus-manufacturing plant was still occupied with war work so the first post-war parlor cars were built by the Pontiac Motor Division. Shown here is PDA-3702-539, built in 1945 for Vancouver Island Coach Lines (VICL). Island Greyhound was strictly a trade name as VICL was never a part of the Greyhound "empire".

The 600 PGA-3702s, 600 PDA-3702s and 100 PD-3302s built were similar to the pre-war versions. They were all constructed by Pontiac Motor Division under authority of the Office of Defense Transportation. Maine Central No. 654 is a 1945 PDA-3702.

The PD-3302s were built in a single batch of 100 in 1945 at Pontiac, Michigan. This photo by J.D. Knowles shows PD-3302-001 in London, Ontario on July 4, 1948. These coaches were commonly referred to as "four bangers" because they were powered by the 4-71 (four cylinders of 71 cubic inches per cylinder) General Motors two-stroke diesel engine. Coach G1727 is shown here as it neared the end of its career with Eastern Canadian Greyhound Lines.

Bus operations by the Bangor & Aroostook Railway lasted for nearly 50 years before ending in early 1984. In 1945, two PD-3302 coaches, No. 500 and No. 502, were delivered along with two of the larger PGA-3702 models. Number 502 is shown in Bangor, Maine.

This is coach PD-2903-001, the first of 400 built from 1946 to 1949. The Blue Line was headquartered in Springfield, Massachusetts and operated south to the coast at New London, Connecticut. In spite of the company name there was no blue in the paint scheme, just black and white. This photo was taken in Willimantic, Connecticut on August 28, 1958.

This Red Star Motor Coaches, Inc. PD-2903 poses for its builder's shot prior to delivery and (unfortunately) before the fleet number was applied. Red Star bought five 2903s in 1946 and four more in 1947. Red Star was purchased by Carolina Coach Company in 1952.

Evergreen Trailways No. 40, a PD-2903, is shown heading to North Bend, Washington. It is one of four 2903s purchased in December 1946. The serials were 078-079 and 136-137.

GM
GENERAL MOTORS
COACH

Model PG-2904

Condensed

SPECIFICATIONS

Overall Length - - - - - - 33'
Body - - - - - - - 32' 8-3/4"
Body Width - - - - - 95-1/4"
Over Rear Tires- - - 94-1/4"
Overall Height
(Loaded) - Front- - 99-7/8"
Headroom
(Aisle Floor) - - - 75-7/8"
(Seat Floor)- - - - 68-7/8"
Aisle Width - - - - - 15"
Floor Height at Aisle
(Loaded)- - - - - - 22-3/8"
Floor Height at Seats
(Loaded)- - - - - - 29-3/8"
Step Height
(Loaded)- - - - - - 15-3/8"
Inside Step Height - - - 7"
Wheelbase - - - - - - 218"
Track -- Front - - - 81-1/2"
Track -- Rear - - - - 73"
Tire Size (Single Front,
Dual Rear) - - - - - 9.00-20" (6" Rims)

CAPACITY Twenty-nine passengers, 24 reclining seats and five passenger non-reclining seat. (See Floor Plan.) Thirty-three passenger seating in non-reclining seats. Optional.

BODY All metal. Aisle recessed 7". Flooring is 9/16"--5 ply plywood, waterproofed.

INSIDE BAGGAGE RACKS Total space approximately 76 cu. ft.

This sales brochure shows typical specifications for the PG-2904 coach.

PG-2904 No. 170 is shown when delivered new in October 1946. This was one of ten purchased by West Ridge at the time, serials 001–010. The Greyhound Corporation acquired West Ridge Transportation Company and its wholly owned subsidiary Buffalo & Erie Coach Corporation in October 1946 and the company was allowed to operate somewhat autonomously for a time.

Once a major carrier serving all four northern New England states, the Boston & Maine Transportation Company (B&M) was the highway subsidiary of the Boston & Maine Railroad, providing intercity, suburban and local city service. Painted a pleasing olive green and cream with narrow red striping, No. 446 was one of 20 PG-2904s purchased in 1946 and 1947. It is shown at Nashua Union Station in November 1954 waiting for a train connection from Boston. Departing at 5:05 p.m. it will carry passengers to a succession of small communities across southern New Hampshire (Milford, Wilton, South Lyndeboro, Greenfield and Peterboro).

In the mid-1950s, the Boston & Maine Transportation Company gradually sold off its routes and coaches. Capital Transit Inc. purchased the Concord, New Hampshire city service, an hourly suburban line between Manchester and Concord and a line haul running north from Concord into the White Mountains. All Capital Transit's original equipment came from the B&M including No. 440, PG-2904-059, built in late 1946 and photographed on July 28, 1959, at The Weirs. It retains the former B&M number and livery of green, cream and red.

*** 37 - PASSENGER ***

INTERCITY TYPE COACH SPECIFICATIONS

LENGTH

Over Bumpers	35'
Over Body	34'-8-3/4"

WIDTH

Over Body at Belt Rail	95-1/4"
Over Rear Tires	95-3/4"

HEIGHT

Overall - Front loaded	111-1/4"
Front empty	113-3/4"
Rear loaded	112-1/4"
Rear empty	114-1/4"
Floor at Aisle - Front loaded	33-5/8"
Front empty	36-1/8"
Rear loaded	34-5/8"
Rear empty	36-5/8"
Floor to Glass Line - Top Minimum	47-11/16"
Bottom Maximum	33-11/16"
Ground to First Step - Entrance loaded	15-1/4"
Entrance empty	17-3/4"

HEIGHT (Cont'd.)

First to Second Step - Entrance	12-7/8"
Second to Floor - Entrance	5-1/2"
Centerline of Bumper - Front loaded	22-3/8"
Front empty	24-7/8"
Rear loaded	19-15/16"
Rear empty	21-15/16"

HEADROOM - At aisle.

Front & Rear	76-1/8"

AISLE WIDTH

Between Seats	15-1/4"

WHEELBASE	239"

OVERHANG - Center of Axle to Bumper

- Front	72-3/4"
- Rear	108-1/4"

TRACK -

Front	80-1/2"
Rear	72-1/2"

TURNING RADIUS - Wheels - Right & Left	44'
Body Corner - Right & Left	46'6"
TIRE SIZE - (Single front, Dual rear)	10.00/20"

BODY CONSTRUCTION - Body proper and understructure, which supports mechanical units are built as a unit forming a rigid structure.

Roof - Aluminum center panels and steel crown panels riveted to pressed steel posts extending from skirt to skirt.

Sides - Aluminum side panels and steel window panels riveted to steel body posts. Rub rails between front and rear wheelhousings. 11" bright finish aluminum appearance panel below windows, each side of body.

Front - Steel front panels riveted to steel corner posts.

Rear - Steel panels riveted to steel posts. Steel engine compartment doors; rear door lift type and side doors swing type allowing maximum accessibility to engine and accessories.

Floor - Aisle recessed 7". Flooring 9/16" - 5 Ply fir plywood bolted to underframe.

Frame - Crossmembers of bulkhead type which also serve as partitions for baggage compartments. Treated plywood securely fastened to bulkheads, serves as baggage compartment floor and protects understructure from road splash, dirt, and corrosive element.

BODY CONSTRUCTION (CONT'D.) - Stepwells of three-step type with bright finish stainless steel risers. Step treads of 3/16" non-skid type.

SEATING ARRANGEMENT - (SEE FLOOR PLAN) - Thirty-seven passengers. Sixteen double reclining seats, eight on each side with five-passenger non-reclining rear lounge seat.

Forty-one passenger seating arrangement with non-reclining seats, optional.

SEATS - Deluxe, reclining chairs with spring cushions and rubber backs, upholstered in mohair. Padded arm rests on aisle and wall sides. Two-position foot rest. All seats equipped with towel bottons and elastic bands. Double seats 38" wide, 17" cushion height. Driver's seat fully adjustable, upholstered in leather, and equipped with full rubber cushion.

DOORS - Manually controlled metal sedan type entrance door opening outward. Door may be locked from outside and reopened by a plunger type release located under windshield. Clear opening through door 24" wide, 77" high.

Emergency door on left side ahead of rear wheels with clear opening of 35-1/2" wide and 49-1/2" high. Hand operated three point lock provided. Red light on instrument panel indicates when lock starts to release.

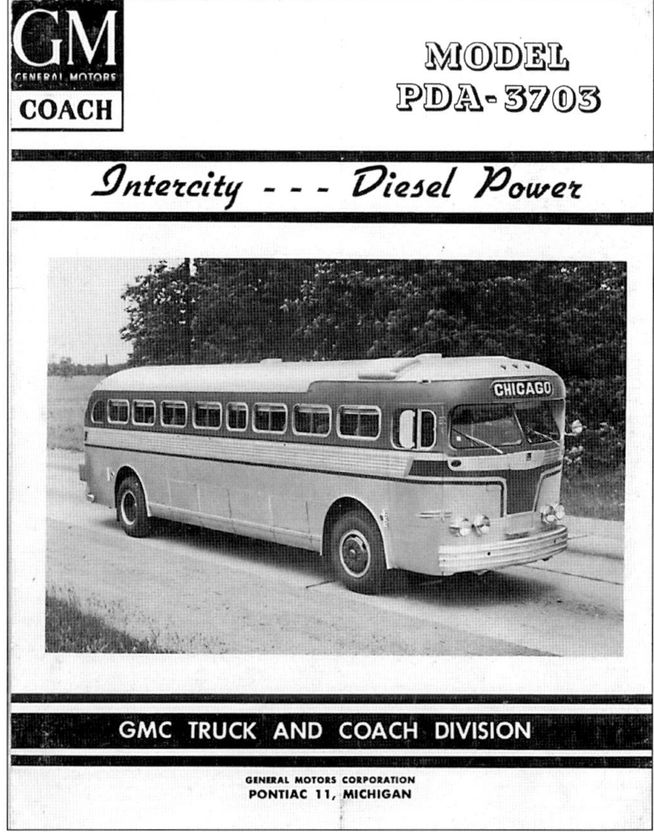

This brochure shows the general specifications for the PDA-3703 which was introduced in 1947.

Vancouver Island Coach Lines, British Columbia, No. 129 is PDA-3703-056. It is lettered for "Island Greyhound" in the 1940s. The PDA-3703 still used the 4-71 General Motors diesel mounted straight in with a four-speed manual transmission. This photo was taken in Victoria, British Columbia.

International Coach Lines, Inc. was a subsidiary of Provincial Transport Company of Montreal, Quebec. International was headquartered in Rumford, Maine and ran between Montreal and Saint John, New Brunswick via Vermont, New Hampshire and Maine. This service was known as "The Short Way" as it was more direct than the route via Quebec and New Brunswick. PDA-3703s No. 4764, No. 4765 and No. 4766 are shown. The company was sold to New England Greyhound in 1953.

Taken at the company's garage in Belmont, Massachusetts is Metropolitan Transit coach No. 90, PDA-3703-002. It was photographed in June 1959 and has received the full silverside treatment. Some operators did this to older coaches to update or modernize their appearance. Note also that the factory fog lights, which were originally mounted inboard of the headlights, have been removed.

The *Silversides* coach was introduced by Yellow prior to World War II and production continued after the war with some minor changes. Before the war there were four models built; the PGG-3701 (Parlor, Gas, Greyhound, 37 seats); the PDG-3701 (Diesel), both of which were 33-foot coaches; the PGG-4101 (Parlor, Gas, Greyhound, 41 seats) and the PDG-4101 (Diesel), which were 35-foot buses. After the war production continued for three years with two models built, the PD-3751 and the PD-4151. They were both 35-foot coaches but had different seat spacing. Crown Coach No. 149 had its builder's photo taken with an incorrect fleet number. The correct fleet number for this coach was actually 152. Crown Coach was not a Greyhound company but was allowed to use the running dog as they did interline work with the 'Hound.

Normally identified with the Greyhound companies and divisions, the *Silversides* were also delivered to other operators, principally those having through service with Greyhound. Short Way Lines of Toledo received PD-3751-1169 in 1949.

The distinctively shaped rear windows of the PD-3751/4151 models were an easy spotting feature of the *Silversides*. The circular Greyhound logo on the rear was dimly illuminated at night while the center amber strip displayed backlit "STOP" lettering when the brakes were applied. Central Greyhound Lines C2244, a PD-3751 built in 1948, awaits a connecting Milwaukee Road train at Columbus, Wisconsin in November 1961. Greyhound provided the service under contract to the railroad, running two daily round trips to Madison, 29 miles to the south.

P-4860 is a 1948 PD-3751 of the Pennsylvania Greyhound fleet. It is shown laying over at Boston in August 1952. Some coaches of this model in the Greyhound fleet were equipped with side destination signs for suburban runs.

A 1947 PD-3751 belonging to Southwestern Greyhound Lines waits for its next assignment behind a PD-4501. The post-war buses were equipped with window shades as shown on S-327 in this 1958 view. *Photo by Ed Thomson*

A typical New York City scene in 1948 finds Central Greyhound Lines C-1557 being directed through an intersection by a traffic officer. The windows and driver's foot vent are closed so the air conditioning is doing its job as the coach leaves New York bound for Schenectady. *Photo by John P. Hoschek*

This PD-3751 was photographed in Elgin, Illinois on July 6, 1958. At that time, Greyhound ran a number of commuter trips between Elgin and Chicago. This coach is laying over for its next hour-and-a-half run back to Chicago. The prefix "C" in the fleet number denotes Central Greyhound Lines.

By late 1962, the PD-3751 *Silversides* had nearly reached the end of its long career with Greyhound. Here in Appleton, Wisconsin in November 1962 a pair is loading Lawrence College students homeward bound for Thanksgiving. Number 2316, formerly Central Greyhound C2316, displays a "Twin Cities" destination sign. The doors of the baggage compartments reveal the ribbed silversiding of the exterior. To open the baggage bay door the driver turned the latch with a hand crank, which was standard practice until the advent of the PD-4104.

When Greyhound purchased hundreds of PD-4104s in the mid- and late-1950s it released for resale its earlier generation of *Silversides*. Small coach operators throughout the U.S. purchased them, including Zephyr Lines of Minneapolis. In April 1963 green and white No. 51, PD-3751-985, has come from Ironwood, Michigan and is loading passengers at Ashland, Wisconsin bound for Hayward, Spooner and Minneapolis. Zephyr also operated from the Twin Cities west to Glenwood, Minnesota and Sisseton, South Dakota.

This is PD-4151-073 ex-Eastern Greyhound Lines E4898 which was originally Great Lakes Greyhound G7038. Manchester Transit purchased it in 1961 for its three-bus charter fleet which was part of its transit operation. The photo was taken in Manchester, New Hampshire in February 1964.

This is a *Silversides* that has been restored by Greyhound. It is PD-4151-014 and is former Pacific Greyhound No. 104 or K104 or P104 depending on the year. Only Great Lakes, Pacific and Teche Greyhound purchased the PD-4151 new.

The largest fleet of PDA-4101s went to American Buslines which, at that time, owned but had not yet absorbed Burlington Transportation, the actual operator of the 26 buses. These were painted maroon and white with the company's stylized eagle and banner emblem which would later be associated with the Trailways "Eagle" bus.

Beginning with the PDA-4101 the ventilators were contained entirely inside, leaving only a flush-mounted screen and two small drain holes on each side of the roof. Asbury Park-New York Transit Corporation had eight of these buses (No. 105-No. 112) which were painted two-tone blue with white tops.

With roots going back to 1914, Peerless Stages is one of America's oldest bus companies. When California State regulation of passenger services came into force in 1917, a number of operators formed the Peerless Auto Stage Association, which was incorporated as Peerless Stages in 1921. PDA-4101-334, fleet No. 239 was the second of two PDA-4101s purchased in 1950. Here it poses in the bright red and yellow paint scheme of the company.

Metropolitan Coach Service PDA-4101-213 is shown in this rear shot with non-standard silversiding. GM's normal treatment for this model was a 12-inch waistband of trim. Metropolitan operated a few city routes in the Belmont suburbs (west of Boston) in addition to running some school bus routes and did a good business in charters as well.

Michaud No. 155 is a PDA-4101 purchased used from Plymouth & Brockton Street Railway. Michaud dates back to 1916 and its logo features a Salem witch with a conical hat riding a broomstick relating to the history of Salem, Massachusetts where the company was based.

Two Greyhound divisions (Dixie and Southwestern) bought the PDA-4101 and this was the first 35-foot , 41-passenger parlor coach offered by GM to customers other than Greyhound. Note the use of a one-piece windshield which was soon changed to a two-piece configuration by most operators because the large windshield tended to crack too easily.

Union Pacific had ten PDA-4101s built in 1949 with 33 seats and a rear baggage compartment which was accessible through an extra door visible behind the right rear wheel. The coaches were used for Union Pacific's train connection service.

This is a coach design in transition. The GM PDA-3704 combined the rounded stern of its predecessor, the PDA-3703, with the modernized front end used on the later PD-4102 and PD-4103. Just 100 PDA-3704s were built, all in 1950. Of these, Peoria-Rockford Bus Company purchased the 96th unit built. In July 1958, Peoria-Rockford's red and silver No. 14 poses in front of the company's Rockford, Illinois garage. Using the fleet name *Silver Arrow* the company operated an extensive route system serving Peoria, Decatur, Springfield, Carbondale (all in Illinois); St. Louis, Missouri; Evansville, Indiana and Milwaukee, Wisconsin.

MODEL
PD-4102

Intercity - - - Diesel Power

GMC TRUCK AND COACH DIVISION

GENERAL MOTORS CORPORATION
PONTIAC 11, MICHIGAN

General specifications for the PD-4102 which was introduced in 1952.

* * * 41-PASSENGER * * *

INTERCITY TYPE COACH SPECIFICATIONS

LENGTH

Over Bumpers	35'
Over Body	34'-9-1/4"

WIDTH

Over Body at Belt Rail	95-5/8"
Over Rear Tires	95-1/4"

HEIGHT - Empty

Overall - Front	115-7/16"
- Rear	115-11/16"
Floor at Aisle - Front	37-13/16"
- Rear	38-1/16"
Floor at Seat Legs - Front	44-3/4"
- Rear	45"
Floor to Glass Line - Top Minimum	47-1/8"
Bottom Maximum	34-1/8"
Ground to First Step	16-1/16"

HEIGHT - Cont'd.

First to Second Step	10-7/8"
Second to Aisle Floor	10-7/8"
Centerline of Bumper - Front	24-3/4"
- Rear	24-3/8"

HEADROOM - At Aisle

Front & Rear	76-1/8"
Seat floor to Package Racks	54-5/8"

AISLE WIDTH

Between Seats	15-1/4"

WHEELBASE 247"

OVERHANG - Center of Axle to Bumper

- Front	72-3/4"
- Rear	100-1/4"

TRACK -

Front	79-1/2"
Rear	70-1/2"

TURNING RADIUS - Wheels - Right & Left 37'6"
Body Corner - Right & Left 41'0"

TIRE SIZE - (Single front, Dual rear) 11.00/20"

BODY CONSTRUCTION - Body proper and understructure, which supports mechanical units are built as a unit forming a rigid structure.

Roof - Aluminum center panels and crown panels riveted to pressed steel posts extending from skirt to skirt.

Sides - Aluminum side and window panels riveted to steel body posts. Aluminum rub rails between front and rear wheelhousings. Panels below belt rail are covered with attractive fluted anodized aluminum panels.

Front - Aluminum front panels riveted to steel corner posts.

Rear - Aluminum engine compartment rear door of lift type retained in open position with telescopic prop; side doors swing type. Aluminum corner panels. Steel collision truss. Engine and radiator shields of aluminum construction mounted horizontally under engine.

Floor - Aisle recessed 7". Flooring 9/16" - 5 Ply fir plywood bolted to underframe.

Frame - Crossmembers of bulkhead type which also serve as partitions for baggage compartments. Treated plywood securely fastened to bulkheads, serves as baggage compartment floor and protects understructure from road splash, dirt, and corrosive elements.

BODY CONSTRUCTION (CONT'D.) - Stepwells - Three step type with bright finish stainless steel risers. Step treads of 3/16" non-skid type. The lower step is retractable functioning in conjunction with door.

SEATING ARRANGEMENT - (SEE FLOOR PLAN) - Forty-one (41) passenger, eighteen (18) double reclining seats, nine (9) on each side with five (5) passenger non-reclining rear lounge seat.

Thirty-seven (37) passenger reclining seats or forty-five (45) passenger non-recliner seats, spaced as shown on floor plan, optional.

SEATS - Deluxe, reclining chairs with spring cushions, head rests, and rubber backs, upholstered in mohair. Padded arm rests on aisle and wall sides. Two-position foot rest. All seats equipped with towel buttons. Double seats 38" wide, 17" cushion height. Driver's seat fully adjustable, upholstered in Koroseal, and equipped with full rubber cushion.

DOORS - Manually controlled metal sedan type entrance door, opening outward. Door may be locked from outside and reopened by a plunger type release located under windshield. Clear opening through door 24" wide, 80-5/8" high. The lower step protrudes as door opens.

Greyhound purchased 35 PDA-4101s and there was only a short run of 4102s built before the introduction of the PD-4103 which incorporated many engineering changes requested by Greyhound. This photo shows the PD-4102 demonstrator.

In 1951 and 1952, the United States Army bought 840 of the military-only model PGA-3301. The coach used a 503-cubic-inch truck engine which was mounted straight in, body panels made with the dies left over from the discontinued PG/PD-29 models and TGH-2708 front ends. In spite of being more transit bus than highway coach, it was designated as a parlor car.

Decked out in Army dark brown, No. 20932429 is seen carrying the troops at Fort Riley, Kansas in June 1960. In spite of the model number (3301), these coaches had 37 non-reclining seats.

Incorporated on May 24, 1921 as the Edwards Motor Transit Co., this company initially provided bus service in Pennsylvania. The company grew by route expansion as well as acquisition and adopted the slogan "Lakes to Sea" when it started running between Buffalo and Washington in 1929. The company was a loyal (but not exclusive) Yellow/GM buyer and this PD-4103 is one of sixteen of this model that it operated.

Quaker City was started in the 1920s to run between Philadelphia and Atlantic City. In 1930, the "Quaker City Limited" service was started to run between Philadelphia and New York. In 1952, the company purchased five PD-4103 coaches, the first diesels for Quaker City. PD-4103-1298 is the last of the five and all had 45 seats in spite of the model number (41).

This is a PD-4103 which was purchased new by the Ray Anthony Orchestra. It was operated by one of the companies in the New York area which specialized in this type of work.

Because of the scarcity of aluminum during the Korean War, many PD-4103s were built without silversiding. Central Greyhound Lines of New York C-1019 crosses the New York Central Railroad in Canandaigua, New York on July 9, 1956. While Greyhound routed most runs over the New York Thruway, two daily round trips still traveled the old state highways and C-1019 westbound to Buffalo took just over 12 hours on its run from Albany.

Vermont Transit Lines No. 663 is PD-4103-1186, a 37-passenger bus built in 1952. It is shown at the old Greyhound terminal in Boston in May 1959. Vermont had six 4103s, three built in 1951 and three built in 1952. Note the fleet name *Green Mountaineer* above the front passenger windows.

This 1951, lavatory-equipped PD-4103 has been assigned to commuter service in San Francisco and is shown in the Greyhound storage yard behind the terminal in Oakland, California. *Photo taken by Andrew R. Harrison in 1967.*

An example of Greyhound's PD-4103s built with full silversiding is Eastern Greyhound Lines E-5111 seen in Portsmouth, New Hampshire in July 1959. By that date, following Greyhound's large intake of PD-4501 Scenicruisers and PD-4104s, these older coaches were relegated to secondary duties. E-5111 bears many scars and dents accumulated during seven years of hard service. "Last Texaco Before Turnpike" proclaims the sign in the background, enticing motorists who have just crossed the bridge from Maine.

General Motors introduced air suspension on the PD-4104, which came out in 1953. This coach stayed in production through 1960 and all 4104s were powered by the transverse mounted 6-71 GM two-stroke diesel coupled to a four-speed manual transmission. Greyhound purchased 1,981 of the 5,065 built. This photo shows a 1954 PD-4104 built for Indian Trails of Michigan.

To Our Friends and Customers:

We take great pleasure extending to you a most cordial welcome to our plant to see how GM coaches are designed, engineered and manufactured.

Coach manufacturing is an intricate, exacting, and progressive industry that must continually meet tomorrow's transportation challenge today. With an abundance of highly-skilled personnel, quality materials, and all the research and engineering resources of our own division and General Motors Corporation behind us, we are confident that we are making for coach operators and passengers alike the finest product of its kind in the world.

It is our never-ending goal to find further new improvements and engineering developments that will keep GM Coach, symbol of quality and efficiency, at the highest peak.

We hope you enjoy your visit.
We are proud to have you as our guest.

Sincerely,
P. J. Monaghan
General Manager

These pages (58-63) depict a promotional brochure released by GM to showcase its coach production operation.

The extensive network of buildings pictured above had its beginning in July, 1927, when ground was broken in a wheat field southeast of Pontiac, Michigan. Today, the entire plant area, which has been growing steadily due to increased demand for the company's trucks and coaches, occupies over 600 acres, with buildings providing over 5 million square feet of floor space. In the center foreground may be seen the Administration Building, and to the right of it Engineering. Over 700,000 square feet of the plant area is devoted to coach assembly, material and inspection alone, with 99% of it on the ground floor. In addition, sheet metal, miscellaneous machining, and engine assembly play a major role in supplying coach assembly. About 3,100 employees are engaged in coach production, engineering and administration. The plant is ideally situated for rail and highway transportation and is within easy distance of the GM Proving Ground, the new Technical Center, and the Corporation's central office in downtown Detroit.

Intercity Coach Production

Paralleling the transit coach line is the parlor model assembly line, where careful coordination is again in evidence.

Component parts such as front and rear roof sections are completely sub-assembled in readiness for timely transfer to the main assembly line.

Materials and accessories are handily placed at the point where they are to be installed.

In virtually every case, employes work standing upright, naturally and comfortably, lessening fatigue and resulting inefficiency.

Sealer is applied to the understructure to insulate the coach against noise, vibration, and to reduce friction.

Installation of floor comes early—(5/8″ plywood—chemically treated for long life). Fluted aluminum side panels are integral with body construction.

Roof sections are assembled on jigs in a pit to enable employes to work more efficiently.

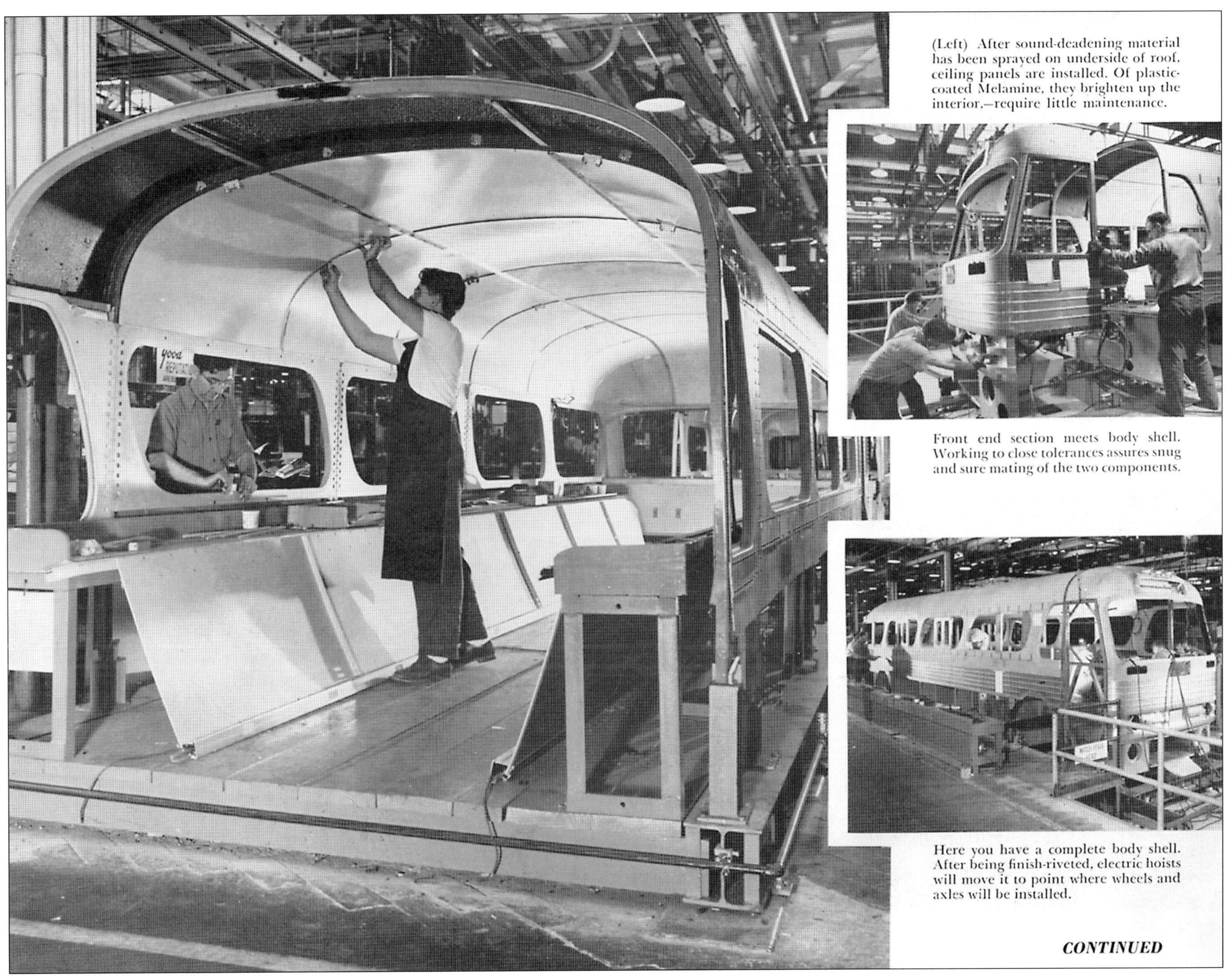

(Left) After sound-deadening material has been sprayed on underside of roof, ceiling panels are installed. Of plastic-coated Melamine, they brighten up the interior,—require little maintenance.

Front end section meets body shell. Working to close tolerances assures snug and sure mating of the two components.

Here you have a complete body shell. After being finish-riveted, electric hoists will move it to point where wheels and axles will be installed.

CONTINUED

With Air Suspension, wheels and axles are connected to body through bellows and rubber-bushed radius rods. Air compartments are integral with body.

Wiring is being completed and doors hung at this station. Major electric wiring is in heavy harness and is located in roof over windows, away from water, dirt or damage.

Wheels and axles are raised from pits on hydraulic lifts and bolted into position. The coach henceforth travels on its wheels.

By means of a turntable, the coach has been transferred to a sidewise conveyor, which will take it through masking, painting, drying, and installation of sash.

Substantial increase in glass area improves visibility for both driver and passengers. Tinted, heat- and glare-resistant safety glass is a standard feature.

Sparkling in their new coat of paint and anodized bright finish aluminum, these models reach the end of the sidewise conveyor. Coach in foreground is on testing rolls. Road tests follow.

Monumental Motor Tours, Inc. was started in the spring of 1925 and was based in Baltimore, the "monumental city". Fleet No. 128 is the second of 26 PD-4104s purchased by the company between 1954 and 1960.

The Public Coordinated Transport Co., Inc. of New Jersey started to buy PD-4104s when they were first introduced. The company purchased 15 non-air conditioned 4104s in 1953 and acquired 77 more over the next years (three were purchased used from Safeway Trails). K606 was one of 25 purchased in 1956. The fleet number letter prefix indicates year of purchase.

Greyhound PD-4104, M-5707, is shown in Carrollton, Kentucky on November 25, 1960. Carrollton is about 25 miles southwest of Cincinnati and was on the scheduled run to Louisville. This coach is en route to Nashville. The prefix "M" in the fleet number denotes a coach operated by Southeastern Greyhound Lines.

Awaiting its next assignment in Raleigh, North Carolina on March 26, 1966, is PD-4104, No. 6069. There were five variations of the "Go Greyhound" motto and this coach has the "For Safety" version. Note the New York World's Fair decal on the entrance door and the collection of license plates on the front of the coach. The letter-prefix divisional identification had been abandoned by this time.

Badger Coaches, Inc. has always had a reputation for running well-maintained equipment such as this PD-4104 shown on a charter trip in Appleton, Wisconsin in March 1962. The company dates back to 1920 and is based in Madison, Wisconsin. As shown on the roof of the coach, its primary route is from Milwaukee to Madison, though the service today operates mainly on I-94.

K608, PD-4104-2255, was operated by Public Service Coordinated Transport (PSCT) of New Jersey. It was one of 92 4104s operated by PSCT. The photo was taken in New York on February 1, 1967.

This one is not a special Greyhound paint scheme but a PD-4104 operated by Crown Coach Company to provide a Kansas City to Joplin, Missouri connection for Southwestern Greyhound Lines. Fleet No. 200 was built in 1956.

The sleek lines of the PD-4104 are shown in this photo of the red, white and blue paint scheme of the Bangor & Aroostook Railroad Co. Highway Division. Shown here in Madawaska, Maine in June 1959, No. 520 is a 1957 PD-4104 en route to Fort Kent.

This PD-4104 was operated by Western New York Motor Lines, Inc., d.b.a. Blue Valley Bus Lines and as Blue Valley Trailways. The company operated out of Buffalo to Batavia and Rochester with some trips going through to Syracuse and Elmira. This photo was taken in December 1959 in Buffalo, New York. The coach is painted the standard Trailways livery of red and cream.

Acadian Lines Limited of Halifax, Nova Scotia, purchased three non-air conditioned PD-4104s, serials 4659-4661, in April 1960. Coach No. 101 is shown at the lookout of Pleasant Bay on the Cabot Trail.

Vancouver Island Coach Lines No. 502, shown on the Malahat Highway in British Columbia in the mid-1950s, is PD-4104-1528, a 45-passenger coach built in 1955.

In 1959, an overdrive clutch assembly became an option on the PD-4104 which gave the bus eight forward speeds. This was shifted hydraulically but was not an automatic transmission. Rather it was a two-speed clutch assembly, which provided a 30 percent overdrive ratio. This was similar to the concept that was used on the *Scenicruisers* when they were built.

Smoother transmission of power . . . reduced engine speed assure longer engine life

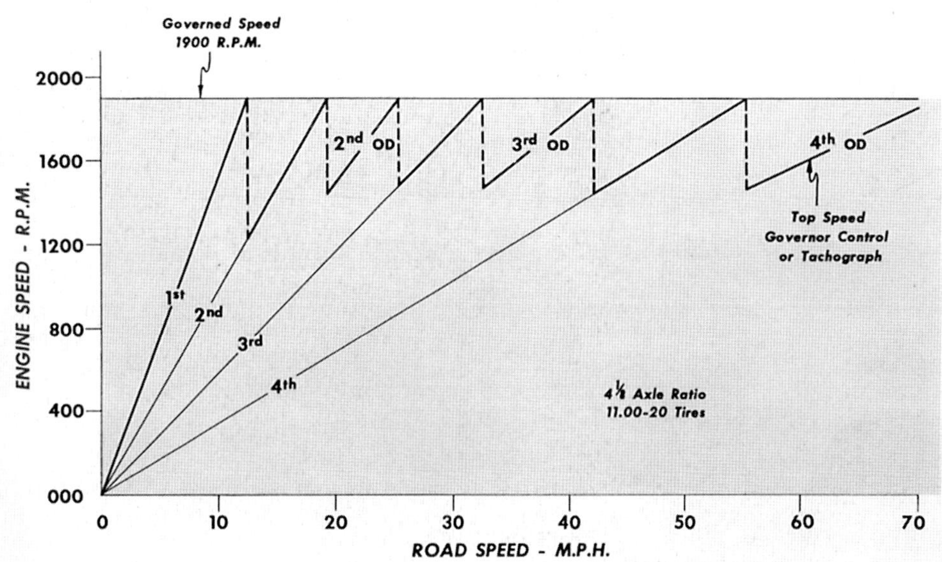

ROAD SPEED vs. ENGINE SPEED

More efficient performance, yet with lowered engine RPM! With Hydrashift, engine can be governed at a maximum speed of 1900 RPM, a factor which should contribute considerably to engine life.

In fact, since about 90% of coach operation will be in fourth overdrive, this means that the engine will operate most of its life around 1600 RPM.

With a 4⅛ axle ratio and 11:00 tires, engine RPM is only 1600 at 62 miles per hour.

For operators not using tachographs, a 2-speed governor is available which regulates engine speed at 1900 RPM in lower gears and 1600 RPM in 4th overdrive.

As the chart above indicates, the driver has a good spread of speed range between drive and overdrive: 6 miles per hour in 2nd . . . 9.5 in 3rd . . . and 16.2 in 4th speed.

Speed ranges between 25 miles per hour and top speed can be operated simply by button shifting, and one gear change.

GMC TRUCK & COACH DIVISION • GENERAL MOTORS CORPORATION

Litho in U.S.

This chart shows the speed ranges which were possible with the "hydra shift" option.

The GX-2 was the experimental 40-foot coach built in 1948 and used mainly to campaign for an increase in allowable length in the states where 35 feet was still the maximum. This deck-and-a-half design led to the production of the famous *Scenicruiser* in 1954.

These coaches were built with dual 4-71 engines driving a single three-speed transmission through a fluid coupling. The clutch assembly provided two speeds so that the coach had six forward gears. This arrangement proved to be somewhat less than successful and all of the remaining *Scenicruisers* were re-powered by the then new 8V-71 in the early 1960s. The new power train used a four speed manual transmission. Eastern Greyhound E-1102 shows the dual radiator arrangement for the two motors.

Dixon, Illinois is 95 miles west of Chicago and the Hotel Dixon once served as a ticket agency on Greyhound's busy Chicago-Des Moines-Omaha main line. On July 7, 1958, Western Greyhound Lines P2400 pauses in Dixon on its long haul from LA to Chicago. In those pre-Interstate highway days, its schedule called for no less than 20 stops just on its trek across Illinois. Note that no less than nine license plates adorn the front of the coach—one for each state between Chicago and Los Angeles.

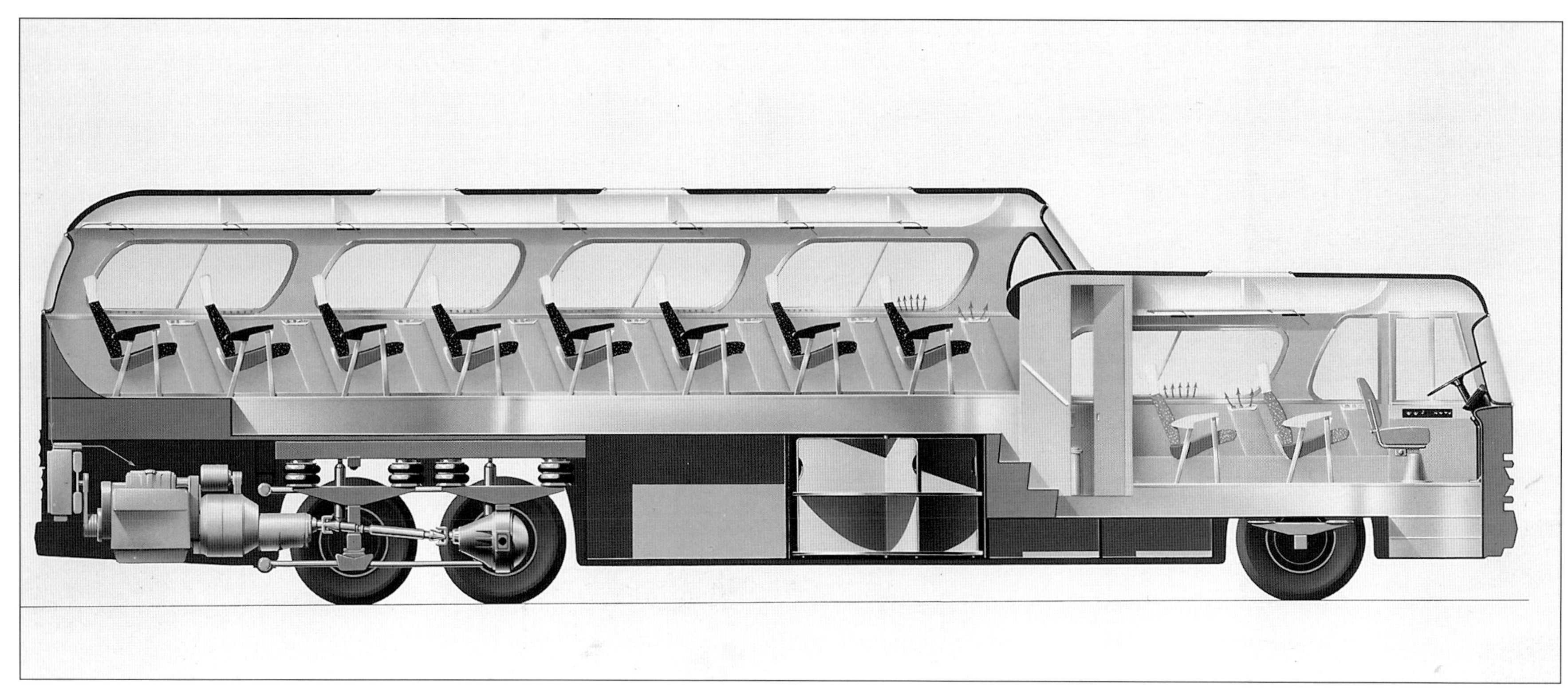

This cutaway of the *Scenicruiser* shows the arrangement of the two diesels mounted to form a 140-degree "V". Note the 43-passenger seating arrangement with the rest room on the lower level, driver's side. The rear axles were a full tandem arrangement (eight tires) but only the front axle of the tandem was driven. The driver could release the air to the suspension on the "tag" axle to shift more weight to the drive axle but the tag wheels did not lift off the ground as they did on the later 4903/4905.

S-157 was a 1955 PD-4501 operated by Southwestern Greyhound. It was about three years old when it was photographed bound for Laredo, Texas. Although the *Scenicruiser* was a durable coach and was popular with its passengers Greyhound did not order more after the initial deliveries were complete. The PD-4104 and later PD-4106 models formed the backbone of the Greyhound deliveries for the next decade. *Photo by Ed Thomson*

PD-4501-514, a 1955 *Scenicruiser*, was numbered GC-13. Originally Great Lakes Greyhound G-7262, it was renumbered when converted to the president's executive car. Note the non-standard A/C screen for stationary or R/V air conditioning. The coach was eventually leased to Anheuser-Busch (Budweiser) and then to the Hartford Insurance Group. It was finally re-seated and returned to line haul service as C-1384.

Although neither of the Canadian Greyhound companies purchased the *Scenicruiser*, the coach was a frequent visitor to some Canadian cities when operated in pool service to Montreal, Quebec; Toronto, Ontario; Winnipeg, Manitoba and Vancouver, British Columbia. Eastern Greyhound Lines E-1096 is shown at the Dorchester Street bus terminal in Montreal in the late 1950s. It operated the schedule back to New York City. When built, the 4501s had non-articulating windshield wipers with a second small wiper blade so that the driver could see his right side mirror. The small wiper arms quickly disappeared and the coaches were eventually retrofitted with the articulated wipers (wiper blade is vertical). Note that E-1096 has one of each type. *Photo by Ed Thompson*

By 1970 Greyhound Lines East No. 4325 was one of the few remaining *Super Scenicruiser* coaches left in active passenger service. The lettering has been updated and the radiator grille has been replaced as part of the conversion to the single General Motors 8V-71 engine that was carried out in the early 1960s. When sold out of Greyhound, many of these coaches found new homes with other line haul and charter operators. This well-designed coach can still be found in use by some operators more than 45 years after its birth and it remains a popular motorhome conversion candidate and collector's item. *Photo by John P. Hoschek*

More than 100 of the PD-4501s in the Greyhound fleet were converted to "combo" coaches after their heyday had passed. A new wall several seat rows forward of the original rear of the passenger compartment separated the passengers from the cargo area, producing a combination freight/passenger vehicle. The *Scenicruiser* had an appropriate axle configuration for this role, although reaching the newly created side cargo door was a stretch. The PD-4501 coaches modified this way were renumbered for easy identification. Fleet No. 0606 is shown in San Francisco in June 1972. *Photo by John P. Hoschek*

It is October 1974 and almost 20 years and two-million miles separate the *Scenicruiser* from the MCI MC-8 behind it. The coaches are pictured here leaving 7th Street in San Francisco. Number 9044 is working a commuter run to Walnut Creek and 1973 MC-8 No. 2228 is on its way to Sacramento.

It is April 9, 1973, and Western Greyhound Lines *Super Scenicruiser* No. 9009 is shown working a commuter trip from San Francisco to Walnut Creek. Not only is it remarkable that these coaches lasted as long as they did in the Greyhound fleet but also that they stayed in front-line service for most of those years and then went on to further use with other commercial operators. *Photo from the collection of Jim Husing*

Michaud No. 182 is a 47-passenger PD-4501 shown in Boston on August 7, 1970. This company purchased two 4501s in 1968 which were the first of this Greyhound exclusive model to be resold to a non-Greyhound company. The witch logo has been replaced with one based on the Interstate highway shield. Michaud used the trade name *Yankee Traveler* on many of its coaches.

Along with its sample *Scenicruiser* GM built a single PD-4901 with the same drive train as the PD-4501 but with all high level seating. Pennsylvania Greyhound ran it for several months between New York and Philadelphia but never bought it. Since the PD-4501 was an exclusive Greyhound design, GM intended to market the 4901 to other operators but there were no buyers so only this one was built.

When the *Scenicruisers* were re-powered with the 8V-71 so was the PD-4901. It was then sold to North Star Lines as their fleet No. 108. The coach is shown leaving Mackinaw City, Michigan in October 1960 in North Star's green and white livery. *Photo from collection of William A. Luke taken by T.C. VanDegrift Jr.*

The Detroit Diesel 8V-71 engine in the PD-4106 provided enough power for the coach as well as the Freon compressor, so that the auxiliary power plant for the air conditioning system on earlier models was no longer required. One disadvantage of this arrangement was that the coach engine had to be left running at rest stops in order to operate the air conditioning, whereas only the small engine would be left running on older air conditioned GM coaches.

Worcester Bus Company No. 140 is PD-4106-3092 photographed in Hampton Beach, New Hampshire on July 26, 1977. Serving the second largest city in Massachusetts, Worcester Bus was another transit company which always fielded several coaches for its charter service. Worcester Bus Company succeeded the former Worcester Street Railway in 1954, although Worcester's electric streetcars had disappeared by 1945.

Mountain View Coach Lines was an old carrier plying the west shore of the Hudson River between Albany, Coxsackie, Saugerties, Kingston and Newburgh. There were several variations of the routes and some trips crossed the Hudson to serve Poughkeepsie. Today, Adirondack Trailways operates Mountain View's former commuter routes, although much reduced in scope. Mountain View No. 97 was a 45-passenger PD-4106 painted light green and white. The mountains of "Mountain" View were the Catskills of New York.

Lake Shore No. 548 is a 1965 PD-4106 with no lavatory, shown at the GM Tech Center on June 8, 1965 with its exterior color of orange and white. Lake Shore traces its history back to 1926 when it ran local bus lines along Lake Erie in Ohio. Ohio Rapid Transit, Inc. was later formed as a holding company for the coaches and various operating companies but Lake Shore System was retained as an operating name.

In 1908, the Martz family started the White Bus Company in the Wilkes-Barre area as an extension to the White auto and truck dealership that they had founded. The White Bus Company became the Frank Martz Coach Company which provided service to Detroit, New York and Philadelphia. This is one of eight 4106s delivered to Martz Trailways in April 1965 (PD-4106-3072-3079 No. 80-No. 87).

Deliveries of the PD-4106 began in March 1961 and they were built until 1965. Shown when new is the 1964, 39-passenger PD-4106-2842 purchased by Burley Bus Lines of Ontario, Canada.

Blue Diamond No. 110 is PD-4106-2938 delivered on February 17, 1965. There were 3,227 4106s built so this was a very late production coach.

Greyhound Lines of Canada bought Canadian Coachways in 1969. With this purchase came a number of GM coaches including this 1965 PD-4106. The coach is shown in Coachways paint in front of the Alberta Legislature in Edmonton (right). It is seen in its new livery outside the Greyhound shop in Calgary, Alberta (above).

The high-level stepped front design was introduced in 1966 on the PD-4107. The 4107 was mechanically the same as the PD-4106 and 1,065 were built in two years but interest fell off when the 40-foot version (PD-4903) was introduced. The coach shown in the photo is the first of the type, PD-4107-001.

This is one of the first PD-4107 *Luxury Liners* to come off the assembly line at GMC Truck & Coach. Tamiami Trail Tours put the coach to work in the popular Trailways Portland, Maine to Miami, Florida pool. Tamiami ran 23 PD-4107s in this pool alongside another 15 supplied by Carolina Coach.

The Greyhound Corporation operated 162 PD-4107s purchased in 1966 and 200 acquired in 1967. This was the last GM parlor coach built for Greyhound as the Motor Coach Industries MC-5 series was finally being produced in quantity. The Greyhound 4107s featured a new exterior paint scheme with a band of red just above "For Pleasure..." which was one of five variations of the "Go Greyhound" motto. The patriotic red, white and blue scheme tied in with the "Discover Greyhound America" campaign as shown by the decal on the entrance door. Southern Greyhound No. 5048 (1966 PD-4107-386) was one of five Greyhound 4107s built with the "Super V" automatic transmission.

Vermont Transit Company, Inc., of Burlington, Vermont V806 is PD-4107-155, a 38-passenger, 1966 coach. It is shown at the loading area of the Central Terminal in Burlington on June 30, 1968 resplendent in its smart green and light yellow colors.

The Greyhound Canada purchase of Canadian Coachways brought six nearly new (1966 and 1967) PD-4107s to the all-MCI fleet. The GMs worked well, especially on the schedules that generated a lot of freight business. The photo (above) in Coachways-style paint is the GM delivery shot of A-503, and the other photograph (right) is of GLOC No. 63 ex-Coachways A-504.

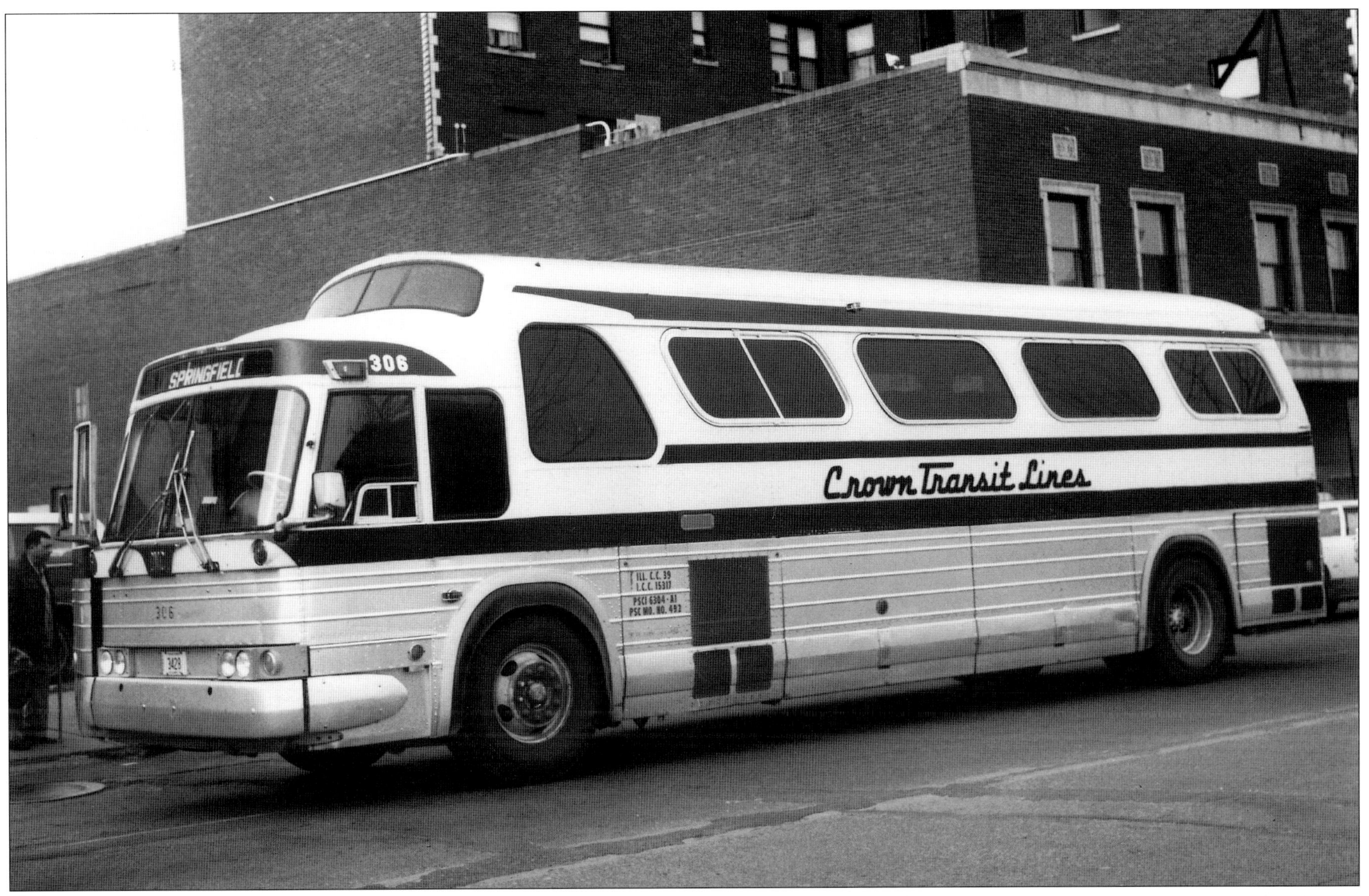

Based in Springfield, Illinois, Crown Transit Lines once operated over 500 miles of intercity routes across central Illinois linking Davenport, Iowa; Springfield, Peoria, Champaign and Terre Haute, Indiana. The company was a reorganization of the former Illinois Transit Lines. On April 5, 1978, Crown No. 306, a PD-4107, was loading at Rock Island, Illinois at 17:20 on its 4 1/2-hour run from Davenport to Springfield, running as trip No. 40. The coach colors are maroon and white.

Much like Greyhound's extensive suburban service out of San Francisco, New Orleans served as a hub for short distance services to communities such as Slidell, Tylertown, Covington, Thibodaux, Huoma and Golden Meadows. The busy Baton Rouge line offered service every one to two hours throughout the day and night. Greyhound based a number of PD-4107s in New Orleans for these routes such as No. 5129 seen on April 10, 1978.

Acadian Lines of Halifax No. 702, a PD-4107, pauses at Peggy's Cove, Nova Scotia in 1967. Peggy's Cove is one of the most photographed sites in North America.

Texas Motor Coaches operated an hourly local service between Dallas, Grand Prairie, Arlington and Fort Worth, plus non-stop turnpike expresses. The local trips took 1 hour 45 minutes and the express trips took only 45 minutes. In April 1978, white, red and blue No. 1744, a PD-4107, is shown ready to depart Fort Worth for Dallas. The large star below the first window promotes the image of the Lone Star State.

Las Vegas-Tonopah-Reno Stage Line, Inc., (LTR) No. 217 is 1970 PD-4108-017, one of nine of this model purchased for use for service on a contract with the Atomic Energy Commission. Starting in 1963, LTR ran an industrial service from the Las Vegas area to Mercury at the southwestern corner of the Nevada test site.

New Mexico Transportation (NMT) ran these PD-4108s in its fleet in the "Land of Enchantment". NMT purchased 15 PD-4107s (No. 223-No. 237) and seven PD-4108s (No. 238-No. 244) before starting to buy MCI buses in 1972. NMT ran pool service with the 'Hound so the company was able to use the Greyhound dog as part of their paint scheme.

New Mexico Transportation was based in Roswell, New Mexico so that when Transportation Manufacturing Corporation (TMC) started to build buses in that city it was inevitable the company would purchase the TMC-8. Motor Coach Industries in Winnipeg was unable to meet the demand for its coaches in the early 1970s so a satellite plant operated as TMC was opened in Roswell.

Grey Goose of Winnipeg, Manitoba is owned by Laidlaw and is therefore part of the Greyhound group of companies. The company runs line-haul service in some of the toughest operating conditions in North America. For many years Grey Goose turned to GM for buses rugged enough to operate over rough roads in brutally cold weather or equally hot weather. "The Goose" had eight 4108s in the fleet as well as an additional 15 of the 40-foot 4905 series.

Saskatchewan Transportation Company provides most of the intercity bus service in the province of Saskatchewan, Canada. Shown in 1972, P8M-4108A-018 is one of eighteen 35-foot GMs the company operated (four 4107s, fourteen 4108s). A change in standard GM model designations resulted in the PD-4108 being called the P8M-4108A starting in 1972.

A transportation institution in the lower Rio Grande Valley of Texas since 1941, Valley Transit Company is based in Harlingen. Its many routes serve Brownsville, Padre Island, McAllen, Mission and Edinburg plus an international line across the border to Reynosa, Mexico and intercity lines north to San Antonio, Corpus Christi and Houston. Blue, white and red No. 502, a P8M-4108A, was one of many GM coaches this company favored over the years. Valley is now controlled by Greyhound Lines.

The history of Jefferson Lines dates back to 1919 when the company started operations in Minnesota. Jefferson first purchased diesel-powered GM coaches in 1941, and this 1968 model PD-4903 was one of four that introduced the 40-foot version of the GM product to the company that year.

The high level GM coaches came to be known as *Buffalo Buses* or *Camels*. GM advertised the buses as having "twelve front seats" as can be seen in this PD-4903 interior shot.

This photo shows the "tag" or idler axle mounted inside the third baggage bay. This axle could not be placed behind the drive axle, as there was not enough room with the GM "angle drive". The extra axle was offered as an option for use in areas that still had an 18,000-pound load limit on the drive axle. The third axle was designed to carry 4,000 pounds. There were also some areas that required three axles for 40-foot coaches. Two-axle models had a baggage bay where the tag axle would have been installed. When not needed the tag wheels tucked up into the bay by means of an air chamber lift system. A smaller tire was used on the tag wheels, 8:00x22.5 vs. 11:75x22.5. The system was removable without altering the coach structure.

Hudson Transit Lines of Mahwah, New Jersey, operating as "Shortline", was a loyal GM buyer until near the end of parlor car production, buying 165 of the 4903/4905 series. H-916 is a 1968 PD-4903, one of sixteen 4903s purchased.

The company modified some of its coaches for sightseeing service as shown by the plastic roof of H-401 pictured at New York's Lincoln Center. Short Line called this coach the *Vistacruiser*.

The last parlor coach purchased new by Greyhound was the PD-4107 but Greyhound Canada ran the 40-foot 4903. Seven PD-4903s equipped with storm windows and tag axles came with the purchase of Canadian Coachways in 1969. A-602 is shown (above) in its delivery photo and GLOC No. 71, ex A-601, is shown (right) repainted in the Greyhound scheme.

Bangor & Aroostook shows off its new PD-4905 fleet No. 550. This is a very early 4905 (PD-4905-008). The 4905 is an updated version of the 4903. The only external difference was the extra engine air-intake louver at the right rear of the coach. All the 4905s were air-conditioned but many operators specified a sliding window at the right front and left rear of the coach. In the case of air-conditioning failure the driver could open these two windows and complete his trip.

The Las Vegas-Tonopah-Reno Stage Line began operating principally as a freight and mail carrier into the Nevada desert north of Las Vegas in 1929 and ran for 60 years. Beginning in 1963, as the result of a contract with the Atomic Energy Commission, LTR became the largest bus company in Nevada. To fulfill this contract, which required up to 70 coaches at its busiest times, LTR started adding GM buses to its fleet. The company eventually had almost 150 GMs before turning to MCI coaches in 1976. Shown at GM in Pontiac is one of three PD-4905s the company purchased in 1970.

CONDENSED SPECIFICATIONS

Body Structure—Body construction is basically aluminum reinforced with steel components. Body proper and under-framing components are built as an integral "monocoque" unit resulting in a chassisless girder-type structure.

Roof—Roof panels and crown panels are painted aluminum riveted to steel posts and strainers respectively. Posts between windows extend from floor line to floor line. Roof areas at front over driver and entrance way has a formed recess which lowers front end silhouette. "Astrolite" between center roof and lower front roof.

Sides—Aluminum side panels and steel window panels riveted to steel upper posts and aluminum lower posts. Lower body around entire coach features fluted side panels anodized with bright finish.

Front—Fluted aluminum panels riveted to steel corner posts. Steel crash panel ⅛" thick provided at driver's position. Steel windshield panel. Fiberglass moulding full width below windshield.

Rear—Rear closure door features fluted aluminum panels, riveted to steel tubular frame. Engine compartment lift type rear door retained in open position with telescopic type prop. Door has permanently attached "T" handle for unlocking which folds into recess in door when not in use.

Floor—Raised passenger floor is flat without recessed aisle or seat platforms. Tiered floor with two steps between the raised floor and driver's floor level. Flooring is ⅝" five ply fir plywood bolted to understructure. Stainless steel seat mounting rails recessed in floor full length of seating area each side of aisle.

Understructure—Two welded steel longitudinal members over each axle with ends attached to transverse aluminum bulkheads. Underfloor space between axles separated by transverse aluminum bulkheads into baggage compartments and space for heating and air conditioning units and fuel tank.

Fenders—Splash Aprons—Exterior front and rear wheel well trim is extruded, anodized aluminum. Molded rubber fenders are furnished at front and rear to control side splash from wheels.

Insulation—Roof, crown panels and body side panels are insulated with glass wool in polyethylene envelopes and pressed fiberglass duct panels. Engine compartment insulated from passenger section by one inch fiberglass pads applied to rear lounge behind seat back and two inch fiberglass pads applied beneath rear seat cushion and inside rear seat riser.

Entrance Door—Manually controlled sedan type entrance door opening outward. Manually controlled operating mechanism completely enclosed. Plunger type release, manually operated, located under windshield unlatches door from outside.

Windshield—Windshield is two piece curved, 15° slanting wrap-around type, divided vertically at center. Glazing is nominal 17/64" Soft-Ray uniform single density laminated safety float glass with .030" plastic interlayer set in black endless rubber channel. Right and left hand sections are interchangeable.

Side Windows—Upper level side windows, four each side, are extruded, anodized aluminum single pane fixed type sash. Window frames are hinged at top and can be pushed out for emergency escape.

Dimensions

	P8M-4108A	P8M-4905A
Length—Glass only	56.25	71.00
Height—Glass only	21.75	21.75
Slide Opening	None	None

Sliding type sash available at additional cost.

Driver's Window—Driver's window is ¼" curved Soft-Ray uniform single density safety float glass glazed with zipper type black rubber channel. It includes a sliding signal section in lower rear corner.

Destination Sign—Built-in type front destination sign is mounted above windshield and glazed with 7/32" solid tempered glass (5⅝" x 71⅜" daylight opening) retained in rubber channel. Illumination provided by four 15 CP bulbs. Mylar single curtain 40" wide and 25 reading each 4" high with white letters on black background furnished as standard equipment.

Mirrors—One interior non-glare type rear view mirror 7" x 10" is mounted on destination sign box door. Two fully adjustable square type exterior mirrors approximately 8½" x 8½" hinged to fold flat against coach. Arm is held firmly in position to prevent movement by vibration.

Windshield Wipers—Two parrallelogram type wipers utilize Sprague "Super Challenger" motors with integral linkage bracket drive. Control valves incorporate self-parking feature and provide speed control from 0 to 110-120 strokes per minute.

Metal Protection—All metal body parts, except anodized aluminum parts, before assembly, are given a thorough eight-stage treatment to inhibit corrosion and insure proper paint adhesion. Parts are thoroughly cleaned with a high temperature cleaning agent, double rinsed and dried, then treated with a controlled zinc phosphate compound solution which produces a chemically clean surface and changes grain structure of metal surface to inhibit corrosion. Complete rinsing with a final acidulated rinse prevents blush rust before priming and prepares surface for good prime bond. Prime paint, a heavy duty zinc chromate for aluminum and steel, is applied to parts, except anodized aluminum, before assembly.

Bright finish aluminum panels, wheelhouses and stepwell are anodized, a process whereby the surface of the metal is converted to aluminum oxide to inhibit corrosion.

Batten compound is used liberally to seal exterior body seams, joints and overlapping panels against entrance of water and dust and to prevent electrolytic corrosion between dissimilar metals.

All bolts, nuts, washers, clamps, clips and like parts are zinc, cadmium plated or phosphate coated to prevent corrosion.

Front Axle—Rockwell-Standard reverse Elliot type with 3½" x 4¾" rectangular tubular axle center and forged hubs. Wheel loads are carried on tapered roller bearings.

Rear Axle—Rockwell-Standard full floating type, heavy duty spiral bevel drive with 63° angle. Housing bowl located to right of axle center line. Axle housing is steel stamping with removable outer end tubes pressed into housing.

Standard rear axle ratio is 4⅛:1 on P8M-4108A and 4⅜:1 on P8M-4905A.

Gear Ratios and Road Speeds

Transmission Gear	Ratio	Angle Drive	Final Drive Ratio P8M-4108A	Final Drive Ratio P8M-4905A
1st	4.28:1	.808	14.27	15.13
2nd	2.50:1	.808	8.33	8.84
3rd	1.50:1	.808	5.00	5.30
4th	1.00:1	.808	3.33	3.54

Road Speed

P8M-4108A-4⅛ Rear Axle @ 1800 rpm

P8M-4905A-4⅜ Rear Axle @ 1900 rpm

1st	15.4
2nd	26.2
3rd	43.6
4th	65.5

Brakes-P8M-4108A—Service brakes are four wheel internal expanding air operated two shoe type on front and rear. Brakes shoes are 5" wide at front and 8" wide at rear.

Brakes-P8M-4905A—Service brakes are four wheel internal expanding air operated two shoe type on front and rear. Brake shoes are 5" wide at front and 10" wide at rear of heavy fabricated steel construction with one piece rollers at cam end and replaceable bushings at anchor pin end. Front and rear anchor pins are chrome plated.

Brake lining is ¾" thick ABB 693-9 bolted to brake shoes with ⅜" bolts with bolt hole in lining plugged with lining material.

Air Brake Controls—Bendix-Westinghouse Type "A" air hose with detachable fittings on rear line. Brake application valve is B-W-E 1 with R-6 relay valve for rear brake application.

Emergency Brake—Emergency brake is air operated Bendix-Westinghouse DD-3 type, consisting of actuators, inversion valve and push-pull control valve mounted at right of driver's seat. DD-3 system satisfies D.O.T. regulations.

Air Compressor—Air compressor is Bendix-Westinghouse "Tu-Flo 600", two cylinder, water cooled unloaded head type with capacity of 14 cu. ft. per minute at 1250 rpm. Compressor is flange mounted to gear train cover and direct driven from left hand camshaft gear. Lubrication is force fed from engine oil system.

Air Tanks—A dual compartment air tank 9½" x 34" and a single air tank 9½" x 16" furnish a capacity of 3250 cu. in. Pressure regulator provided in air line between the single tank (9½" x 16") and suspension, air horn, air gauge, etc. systems. insures adequate pressure for brake application and prevents loss of air in braking system in the event of leakage in the above auxiliary air system units.

Instrument Panel—Control and instrument panel located on dash in front of driver is tilted at 28° angle from vertical. To the right of the steering column a panel is designed to accept new electronic standard speedometer with odometer, Argo tachograph, or a Sangamo tachograph. The panel left of the steering column has an air gauge, oil pressure gauge, temperature gauge, voltmeter, and provisions for the optional dash mounted fuel gauge. Each panel insert can easily be removed individually for gauge and switch maintenance. Telltale lights are located across the top of the panel.

The following pages outline the condensed specifications for the P8M-4108A and the P8M-4905A.

DIMENSIONAL DATA	P8M-4108A	P8M-4905A
LENGTH OVER BUMPERS	35′	39′11⅞₄″
WIDTH	95.76″	95.76″
HEIGHT—Overall—Front	131.50″	131.50″
—Rear	131.58″	131.58″
FRONT STEP HEIGHT		
Ground to First Step	15.42″	15.42″
First to Second Step	7.38″	7.38″
Second to Third Step	7.38″	7.38″
Third Step to Floor	7.38″	7.38″
WHEELBASE	259.50″	318.54″
HEADROOM	75.75″	75.75″
AISLE WIDTH—Between Seats	14.25″	14.25″
DOOR CLEARANCE OPENING		
Entrance	25.00″	25.00″
TURNING RADIUS		
Front Tire—R.H. Turn	39′6″	45′0″
—L.H. Turn	39′6″	45′0″
Front Body Corner—R.H. Turn	43′6″	49′0″
—L.H. Turn	43′6″	49′0″
TIRE SIZE		
Front	12.00/22.5-14 P.R.	12.50/22.5-14 P.R.
Dual Rear	12.00/22.5-14 P.R.	12.50/22.5-14 P.R.
Third Axle (Optional)	Not required	8.00/22.5-10 P.R.

Up to 403 cubic feet of underfloor baggage space

Whether it's package express, or tour group's baggage, or athletic gear, there's never too much baggage space. GMC offers up to 403 cubic feet in its highway models. In the P8M-4108A and the P8M-4905A with three axles, there are 290 cubic feet of space. With two axles, the P8M-4905A has an extra compartment containing 113 cubic feet. All compartments are full coach width, 87″ wide by 39″ high and are equally accessible from either side. Doors are pantograph type, requiring little effort to lift. They rise "vertically", requiring minimum swing-out space in close quarters, and park high up and out of the way when fully opened. All compartments, when closed, are completely sealed against dust, dirt, moisture and road splash. Floors are transversely ribbed and reinforced with longitudinally corrugated sheet aluminum. Optional shelves are shown in the picture across the page. For small packages, light luggage, etc., interior package racks provide 158 cu. ft. of space in Model P8M-4905A, 138 cu. ft. in P8M-4108A.

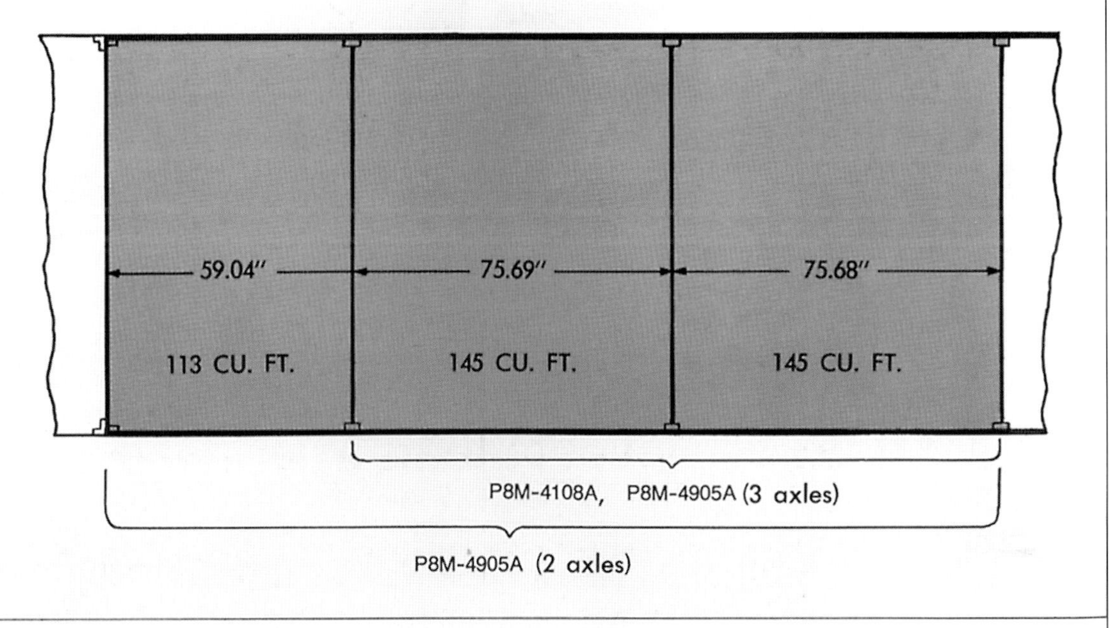

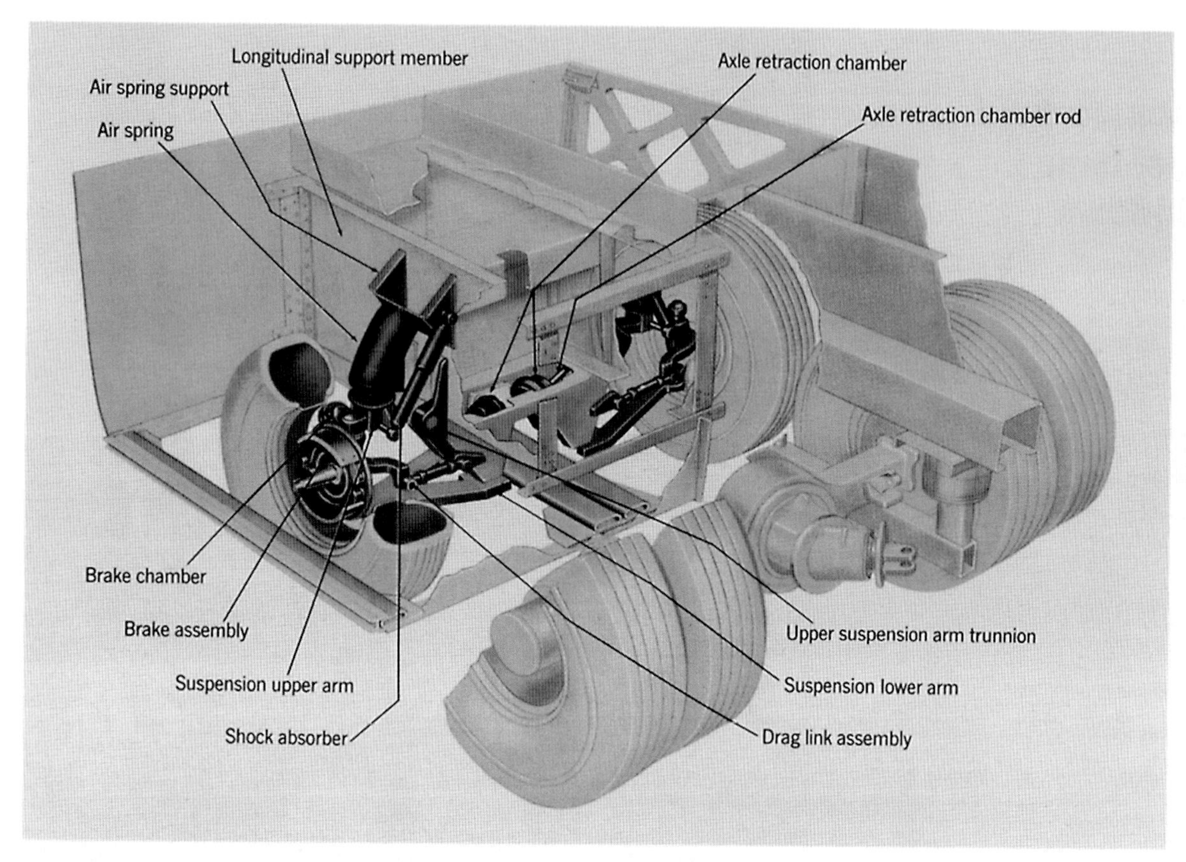

Optional third axle

To permit operation in states with less than 20,000 pounds axle loading, a third axle is optionally available in model P8M-4905A.

The system is expressly designed with two important features: One, it is fully retractable. For less than full load conditions, it may be retracted by the driver at the flick of a button. Air pressure lifts and holds the wheels off the road. Two, it is removable. The entire installation can be dismantled without affecting the coach body structure, should new laws render the axle unnecessary.

Designed to support in excess of 4,000 pounds of load, it brings the main rear axle weight well below the 18,000 pound limit presently legal in a number of states, and also satisfies the requirement of three axles for 40′ vehicles.

Here's another advantage. Over a period of time, and extensive travel across states with varying weight and axle regulations, there is potential for savings in taxes and toll charges with the retractable axle.

With fully independent suspension, the axle is linked with the coach body through air springs, shock absorbers and swing-type arms. Proper alignment is maintained through adjustable control rods. Air brakes, with 202 square inches of effective braking area, contribute to vehicle stopping.

Since the installation occupies what would be the third baggage compartment in the standard vehicle, baggage doors are retained and the system is concealed from view. The long, sleek 2-axle appearance of the coach is maintained. With shields, splash aprons and undercoating, the compartment is fully protected against exterior road and weather conditions.

Other popular options include fluid fan drive . . . larger fuel tank . . . double glazed windows

Graham-White moisture ejector valve on air brake system

Engler hubodometer mounted on right rear wheel.

Dual rear shock absorbers

Ether capsule cold weather starting aid

Perry water filter

Fluid fan drive

Silicone water hoses in engine compartment and heating system

Kysor air-operated radiator winterfront

Automatic engine shutoff for engine overheat and low oil pressure with overrule switch

Fuel tank gauge mounted on dash or at filler neck

Stereo tape system with radio, public address and six or eight ceiling mounted speakers

Tachographs mounted in dash or on lavatory wall

Sliding type sash

Thermopane side windows for extreme cold weather operation

Removable full width baggage compartment shelves

165-gallon fuel tank

Key-type locks on entrance door, baggage doors and battery compartment doors

Right hand padded sun visor

One tow eye at center rear of coach

Pedestal-mounted seats

Black satin-finish exterior sash

Astrolite panel replacing glass

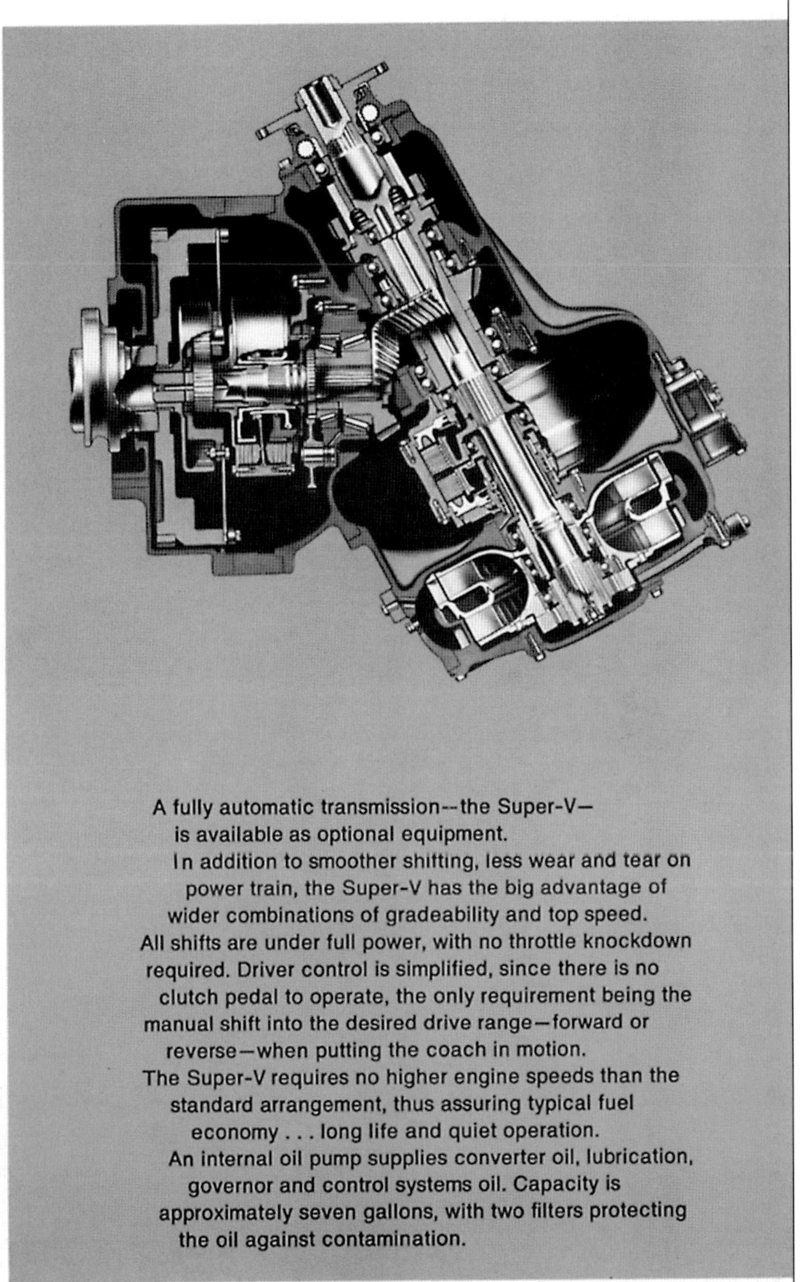

A fully automatic transmission--the Super-V—is available as optional equipment. In addition to smoother shifting, less wear and tear on power train, the Super-V has the big advantage of wider combinations of gradeability and top speed. All shifts are under full power, with no throttle knockdown required. Driver control is simplified, since there is no clutch pedal to operate, the only requirement being the manual shift into the desired drive range—forward or reverse—when putting the coach in motion. The Super-V requires no higher engine speeds than the standard arrangement, thus assuring typical fuel economy . . . long life and quiet operation. An internal oil pump supplies converter oil, lubrication, governor and control systems oil. Capacity is approximately seven gallons, with two filters protecting the oil against contamination.

CONDENSED SPECIFICATIONS

An additional air tank 9½" x 16" with a capacity of 1000 cu. in. furnishes air for Bendix-Westinghouse DD-3 parking and emergency brake system. The total capacity of the dual tank, and the two single tanks is 4250 cu. in.

Air Lines—All metal air lines are annealed copper tubing covered with loom except for main one inch OD air line between compressor and first air tank which is not loomed to insure adequate cooling of air between compressor and first tank. Rubber grommets are used at all points where air lines pass through bulkheads.

Air Suspension—Vertical loads are taken directly by eight air springs, four, nine inch diameter at front and four 10" diameter at rear. Air springs are rolling lobe, single convolution type made of two ply nylon tire fabric, weather resistant neoprene and mounted directly to frame members which form integral part of coach understructure. Air pressure in air springs is varied automatically in proportion to vehicle load by three height control valves—one at front and two at rear. Height control valves maintain constant vehicle height.

Radius Rods—Four radius rods at each axle control lateral and longitudinal position of axles and transmit driving and braking forces from axles to coach body.

Shock Absorbers—Aircraft type direct, double acting shock absorbers are used at both sides of front and rear axles to control rebound and further cushion ride. Shock absorbers are telescoping type of welded construction.

P8M-4108A—Steering—Manual steering system consists of steering column and bevel gear assembly, drive shaft, axle mounted steering gear assembly, drag link and related front axle parts. Steering wheel is 22" diameter of white molded plastic equipped with two puller screw holes.

P8M-4905A—Power Steering—The P8M-4905A coach is equipped with power steering as standard equipment. The power steering system provides automatic hydraulic assistance to the turning effort.

Propeller Shaft—Spicer 3½" diameter tubular steel shaft with Series 1700 heavy duty needle bearing universal joints between transmission and rear axle. Slipjoint at transmission end compensates for vertical movement at rear axle.

Wheels—Tires—Wheels are Firestone 22.5 x 8.25 steel spoke with five ventilating holes in disc. Rims are drop center for tubeless tires. All wheels have 6⅝" offset. Dual spacing of rear wheels is 13¼". Wheels are piloted on hub studs and load is transferred from studs to wheel. One spare wheel is furnished in underfloor compartment at front of coach with access through hinged front bumper and compartment door.

Power Plant—The engine, clutch, angle drive and transmission form a unit power plant which is mounted transversely in rear of coach. The unit power plant has a three point rubber mounting—front, trunnion type; rear, two point cradle type—to an engine cradle assembly. The engine cradle is mounted to the engine bulkhead at two locations, also two cradle support hangers are attached to roof strainer brackets. The complete unit may be quickly removed with a dolly.

Cooling System—Water pump is centrifugal type driven from right hand camshaft with output of 120 gallons per minute at 1800 engine rpm. Capacity of engine radiator with heating system is approximately 101 quarts. Radiator core thickness is 3¼" and frontal area is approximately 1060 sq. in. Radiator is installed in fixed position at left rear corner of coach.

Air Cleaner—Engine air enters through louvered and screened opening at right rear corner at belt rail and is passed through small plenum chamber to a single large oil bath air cleaner supported from engine compartment top panel, then through air silencer to blower. Air cleaner element is removable for cleaning.

Exhaust System—Single 18" x 28" muffler is mounted vertically in center of coach in compartment ahead of engine bulkhead. Single tail pipe outlet exhausts below bumper at left rear corner of coach.

Fuel System—One 140 gallon fuel tank equipped with "Ventalarm" which produces an audible whistle until tank is full. Tank is constructed of terneplate to prevent rusting and is shaped and baffled to prevent excessive surging. Tank is mounted transversely in first bay behind front axle.

Clutch—GM three plate wet clutch with three 15" driven members. Driven members are faced with composition paper and felt material with a resin binder. Conical spring provides load force and release is by manual application of foot pedal which is connected to clutch release lever through rod type linkage.

Angle Gears—Located between the clutch and transmission, the 63° angle gears are pressure lubricated by an engine driven pump. Angle gear ratio is .808:1.

Transmission—Spicer 7145 VK constant mesh four speed mechanical transmission is located in drive line between angle gears and propeller shaft.

Transmission ratios are:

1st	4.28:1
2nd	2.50:1
3rd	1.50:1
4th	1.00:1
Reverse	3.56:1

These ratios do not include .808:1 angle drive gear ratio.

Starting Motor—Delco-Remy starting motor operated by a solenoid on the starter and controlled by start button on driver's and engine compartment control panels. Starter incorporates sprag type over-running clutch drive with totally enclosed shift lever, sealed to prevent entrance of dirt and oil.

Generator—Delco-Remy 24-volt, oil-cooled, AC type generator driven through step-up gear drive from right hand camshaft. Generator produces 70 amperes at 465 engine rpm and reaches output of 260 amperes at approximately 1000 engine rpm. Transistor type voltage regulator controls voltage electronically through transistors and diodes, eliminating necessity for any moving parts.

Batteries—Two 12-volt, Delco 8DR205-WC3, 27-plate end terminal type batteries connected in series provide 24 volts. Total capacity of batteries is 205 ampere hours at 20-hour rate.

Interior Lighting—Reading lights are installed on an electrically wired track recessed in the aisle edge of the package racks and can be removed and reinstalled in any position along track to accommodate variations in seating plans. Two reading light fixtures are provided at each two passenger seat starting with second seat and two fixtures over the rear lounge seat. General lighting is provided by 6 CP bulbs (14 on 4905A and 12 on 4108A) mounted in package rack hangers near ceiling. The general lights are controlled by a toggle type switch mounted on instrument panel.

Exterior Lighting—Dual 12-volt headlamps on each side of coach front are sealed beam units, flush mounted in fiberglass housing with chrome plated trim rings. The high and low beam is controlled by a foot operated dimmer switch. Telltale light on instrument panel indicates when headlamps are on high beam. Front directional signals with 4" diameter amber lens are mounted in right and left hand body corners just below windshield in fiberglass housing. Rear directional signals are 7" in diameter with red lens of "Lexan" material, and are located at left and right rear body corners. Armored type side directional signals with Beehive type amber lens are located on each side of coach near front just forward of wheelhousings.

Combination marker and clearance lights attached to body at each corner of roof and on each side of roof at center. Front and side lights have amber lens and rear have red lens. Identification lights (three lamp cluster) are mounted at center front and center rear of roof crown. Front lights with amber lens are recessed in roof crown above destination sign—rear lights with red lens are attached to rear roof projection above rear window.

Horn—Three horns are provided, two Delco-Remy electrical and one Hadley air operated, located beneath right front corner under step.

Signal System—Electric chime located under dash to left of driver is actuated by two pull switches, one on each side at front.

(Specifications subject to change without notice.)

GMC TRUCK & COACH

Division of General Motors Corporation

Pontiac, Michigan

In Canada: Diesel Division of General Motors London, Ontario

Gray Coach of Toronto, Ontario is now part of the Greyhound Canada Transportation Corporation, but when this photo was taken the company was the Highway Division of the Toronto Transit Commission (TTC). Number1425 is one of fifteen 4905s that the TTC purchased in 1974. They were serial numbers P8M-4905A-610 to -624 and fleet numbers 1420 to 1434.

Saskatchewan Transportation Company (STC) is headquartered in Regina, Saskatchewan. The company purchased 14 P8M-4905As in 1976 to provide line-haul service throughout the province. STC carries a lot of freight, especially in the North, and the 4905s were ideal for this work.

Based in Bowling Green, Kentucky, Tennessee Trailblazers operated several intercity routes in central Tennessee and Kentucky. The company's charter business took its coaches further afield to destinations such as Atlanta, Georgia where green, yellow and white P8M-4905A No. 735 is seen in April 1978. The company called its coaches *Funliners* as can be seen just below the driver's side window. The third bin door on No. 735 does not access a baggage bay but rather the idler axle whose tire is just visible ahead of the rear or drive wheels.

Most would not suspect that Triangle Transportation No. 62 is a three-axle P8M-4905A. When the idler axle is fully retracted, one must peer underneath the coach just forward of the rear axle to see the bottom of the tire. In August of 1987, Triangle No. 62, painted a three tone blue and white, was on its way from Grand Forks, North Dakota to Duluth, Minnesota and is taking on passengers in Crookston, 26 miles into its 265-mile route.

Wisconsin-Michigan Coaches (WMC) No. 119, a two-axle, P8M-4905A, enjoys a 25-minute rest stop at Steven's Point, Wisconsin in August 1987, while on a Milwaukee to Duluth run. Connections could be made here with Hiawatha Coaches to La Crosse and with Greyhound to Minneapolis, Madison, Green Bay and Chicago. At that time, WMC was a member of the National Trailways Bus System but few of its coaches were repainted in Trailways colors.

The drivers loved them, the passengers loved them and the mechanics loved them. As long as they were in production, GMs were bought by Grey Goose Bus Lines of Winnipeg, Manitoba; heart and soul of MCI country. P8M-4905A-1413 is one of six bought in 1976 and one of fifteen 40-foot GMs the company eventually operated.

Part of the Trailways system, Pine Hill Kingston Bus Corporation of New York bought P8M-4905A-193 in 1972 as their fleet No. 72701. The sliding window at the right rear was installed to make it easier to service and to clean the rest room.

Voyageur Colonial Limited (Ontario) No. 1552 P8M-4905A-1743 is shown at Fleet Carrier Corporation in Pontiac, Michigan on July 2, 1977. Note that the front of the raised section of the roof is painted white. It was later repainted black.

By 1980 steadily decreasing demand for its aging line of parlor coaches coupled with a change in corporate direction prompted the General Motors Truck & Coach Division to exit the highway coach business. In the final two years of production the 40-foot model was re-designated as the H8H-649. After producing 125 examples in 1979 and 118 in 1980, General Motors delivered Eastshore Lines No. 340 (serial number 233) as the very last GM parlor car built. *Photo by Warren K. Miller courtesy of the Motor Bus Society*

General Motors did have plans to continue highway coach production and built this bus as the prototype for the next model. It was never given a model designation but was known to GM personnel as the "Titan II". Warren Miller tried to buy the coach but GM was not selling and it was eventually parted out by Blitz Bus in Chicago.

AMERICAN CULTURE

- *Coca-Cola: A History in Photographs 1930-1969* ISBN 1-882256-46-8
- *Coca-Cola: Its Vehicles in Photographs 1930-1969* ISBN 1-882256-47-6
- *Phillips 66 1945-1954 Photo Archive* ISBN 1-882256-42-5

AUTOMOTIVE

- *AMX Photo Archive: From Concept to Reality* ISBN 1-58388-062-3
- *Auburn Automobiles 1900-1936 Photo Archive* ISBN 1-58388-093-3
- *Camaro 1967-2000 Photo Archive* ISBN 1-58388-032-1
- *Checker Cab Co. Photo History* ISBN 1-58388-100-X
- *Chevrolet Station Wagons 1946-1966 Photo Archive* ISBN 1-58388-069-0
- *Classic American Limousines 1955-2000 Photo Archive* ISBN 1-58388-041-0
- *Corvair by Chevrolet Experimental & Production Cars 1957-1969, Ludvigsen Library Series* ISBN 1-58388-058-5
- *Corvette The Exotic Experimental Cars, Ludvigsen Library Series* ISBN 1-58388-017-8
- *Corvette Prototypes & Show Cars Photo Album* ISBN 1-882256-77-8
- *Early Ford V-8s 1932-1942 Photo Album* ISBN 1-882256-97-2
- *Ferrari- The Factory Maranello's Secrets 1950-1975, Ludvigsen Library Series* ISBN 1-58388-085-2
- *Ford Postwar Flatheads 1946-1953 Photo Archive* ISBN 1-58388-080-1
- *Ford Station Wagons 1929-1991 Photo History* ISBN 1-58388-103-4
- *Imperial 1955-1963 Photo Archive* ISBN 1-882256-22-0
- *Imperial 1964-1968 Photo Archive* ISBN 1-882256-23-9
- *Javelin Photo Archive: From Concept to Reality* ISBN 1-58388-071-2
- *Lincoln Motor Cars 1920-1942 Photo Archive* ISBN 1-882256-57-3
- *Lincoln Motor Cars 1946-1960 Photo Archive* ISBN 1-882256-58-1
- *Nash 1936-1957 Photo Archive* ISBN 1-58388-086-0
- *Packard Motor Cars 1935-1942 Photo Archive* ISBN 1-882256-44-1
- *Packard Motor Cars 1946-1958 Photo Archive* ISBN 1-882256-45-X
- *Pontiac Dream Cars, Show Cars & Prototypes 1928-1998 Photo Album* ISBN 1-882256-93-X
- *Pontiac Firebird Trans-Am 1969-1999 Photo Album* ISBN 1-882256-95-6
- *Pontiac Firebird 1967-2000 Photo History* ISBN 1-58388-028-3
- *Rambler 1950-1969 Photo Archive* ISBN 1-58388-078-X
- *Stretch Limousines 1928-2001 Photo Archive* ISBN 1-58388-070-4
- *Studebaker 1933-1942 Photo Archive* ISBN 1-882256-24-7
- *Studebaker Hawk 1956-1964 Photo Archive* ISBN 1-58388-094-1
- *Studebaker Lark 1959-1966 Photo Archive* ISBN 1-58388-107-7
- *Ultimate Corvette Trivia Challenge* ISBN 1-58388-035-6

BUSES

- *Buses of ACF Photo Archive* ISBN 1-58388-101-8
- *Buses of Motor Coach Industries 1932-2000 Photo Archive* ISBN 1-58388-039-9
- *Fageol & Twin Coach Buses 1922-1956 Photo Archive* ISBN 1-58388-075-5
- *Flxible Intercity Buses 1924-1970 Photo Archive* ISBN 1-58388-108-5
- *Flxible Transit Buses 1953-1995 Photo Archive* ISBN 1-58388-053-4
- *GM Intercity Coaches 1944-1980 Photo Archive* ISBN 1-58388-099-2
- *Greyhound Buses 1914-2000 Photo Archive* ISBN 1-58388-027-5
- *Mack® Buses 1900-1960 Photo Archive** ISBN 1-58388-020-8
- *Prevost Buses 1924-2002 Photo Archive* ISBN 1-58388-083-6
- *Trailways Buses 1936-2001 Photo Archive* ISBN 1-58388-029-1
- *Trolley Buses 1913-2001 Photo Archive* ISBN 1-58388-057-7
- *Yellow Coach Buses 1923-1943 Photo Archive* ISBN 1-58388-054-2

EMERGENCY VEHICLES

- *The American Ambulance 1900-2002: An Illustrated History* ISBN 1-58388-081-X
- *American Funeral Vehicles 1883-2003 Illustrated History* ISBN 1-58388-104-2
- *American LaFrance 700 Series 1945-1952 Photo Archive* ISBN 1-882256-90-5
- *American LaFrance 700 Series 1945-1952 Photo Archive Volume 2* ISBN 1-58388-025-9
- *American LaFrance 700 & 800 Series 1953-1958 Photo Archive* ISBN 1-882256-91-3
- *American LaFrance 900 Series 1958-1964 Photo Archive* ISBN 1-58388-002-X
- *Classic Seagrave 1935-1951 Photo Archive* ISBN 1-58388-034-8
- *Crown Firecoach 1951-1985 Photo Archive* ISBN 1-58388-047-X
- *Fire Chief Cars 1900-1997 Photo Album* ISBN 1-882256-87-5
- *Hahn Fire Apparatus 1923-1990 Photo Archive* ISBN 1-58388-077-1
- *Heavy Rescue Trucks 1931-2000 Photo Gallery* ISBN 1-58388-045-3
- *Imperial Fire Apparatus 1969-1976 Photo Archive* ISBN 1-58388-091-7
- *Industrial and Private Fire Apparatus 1925-2001 Photo Archive* ISBN 1-58388-049-6
- *Los Angeles City Fire Apparatus 1953-1999 Photo Archive* ISBN 1-58388-012-7
- *Mack Model C Fire Trucks 1957-1967 Photo Archive** ISBN 1-58388-014-3
- *Mack Model L Fire Trucks 1940-1954 Photo Archive** ISBN 1-882256-86-7
- *Maxim Fire Apparatus 1914-1989 Photo Archive* ISBN 1-58388-050-X
- *Navy & Marine Corps Fire Apparatus 1836 -2000 Photo Gallery* ISBN 1-58388-031-3
- *Pierre Thibault Ltd. Fire Apparatus 1918-1990 Photo Archive* ISBN 1-58388-074-7
- *Pirsch Fire Apparatus 1890-1991 Photo Archive* ISBN 1-58388-082-8
- *Police Cars: Restoring, Collecting & Showing America's Finest Sedans* ISBN 1-58388-046-1
- *Saulsbury Fire Rescue Apparatus 1956-2003 Photo Archive* ISBN 1-58388-106-9
- *Seagrave 70th Anniversary Series Photo Archive* ISBN 1-58388-001-1
- *TASC Fire Apparatus 1946-1985 Photo Archive* ISBN 1-58388-065-8
- *Volunteer & Rural Fire Apparatus Photo Gallery* ISBN 1-58388-005-4
- *W.S. Darley & Co. Fire Apparatus 1908-2000 Photo Archive* ISBN 1-58388-061-5
- *Ward LaFrance Fire Trucks 1918-1978 Photo Archive* ISBN 1-58388-013-5
- *Wildland Fire Apparatus 1940-2001 Photo Gallery* ISBN 1-58388-056-9
- *Young Fire Equipment 1932-1991 Photo Archive* ISBN 1-58388-015-1

RACING

- *Chaparral Can-Am Racing Cars from Texas, Ludvigsen Library Series* ISBN 1-58388-066-6
- *Cunningham Sports Cars, Ludvigsen Library Series* ISBN 1-58388-109-3
- *Drag Racing Funny Cars of the 1960s Photo Archive* ISBN 1-58388-097-6
- *Drag Racing Funny Cars of the 1970s Photo Archive* ISBN 1-58388-068-2
- *El Mirage Impressions: Dry Lakes Land Speed Racing* ISBN 1-58388-059-3
- *GT40 Photo Archive* ISBN 1-882256-64-6
- *Indy Cars of the 1950s, Ludvigsen Library Series* ISBN 1-58388-018-6
- *Indy Cars of the 1960s, Ludvigsen Library Series* ISBN 1-58388-052-6
- *Indy Cars of the 1970s, Ludvigsen Library Series* ISBN 1-58388-098-4
- *Indianapolis Racing Cars of Frank Kurtis 1941-1963 Photo Archive* ISBN 1-58388-026-7
- *Juan Manuel Fangio World Champion Driver Series Photo Album* ISBN 1-58388-008-9

- *Lost Race Tracks Treasures of Automobile Racing* ISBN 1-58388-084-4
- *Mario Andretti World Champion Driver Series Photo Album* ISBN 1-58388-009-7
- *Mercedes-Benz 300SL Racing Cars 1952-1953, Ludvigsen Library Series* ISBN 1-58388-067-4
- *Novi V-8 Indy Cars 1941-1965, Ludvigsen Library Series* ISBN 1-58388-037-2
- *Porsche Spyders Type 550 1953-1956, Ludvigsen Library Series* ISBN 1-58388-092-5
- *Sebring 12-Hour Race 1970 Photo Archive* ISBN 1-882256-20-4
- *Vanderbilt Cup Race 1936 & 1937 Photo Archive* ISBN 1-882256-66-2

RAILWAYS

- *Chicago, St. Paul, Minneapolis & Omaha Railway 1880-1940 Photo Archive* ISBN 1-882256-67-0
- *Chicago & North Western Railway 1975-1995 Photo Archive* ISBN 1-882256-76-X
- *Great Northern Railway 1945-1970 Volume 2 Photo Archive* ISBN 1-882256-79-4
- *Great Northern Railway Ore Docks of Lake Superior Photo Archive* ISBN 1-58388-073-9
- *Illinois Central Railroad 1854-1960 Photo Archive* ISBN 1-58388-063-1
- *Milwaukee Road 1850-1960 Photo Archive* ISBN 1-882256-61-1
- *Milwaukee Road Depots 1856-1954 Photo Archive* ISBN 1-58388-040-2
- *Show Trains of the 20th Century* ISBN 1-58388-030-5
- *Soo Line 1975-1992 Photo Archive* ISBN 1-882256-68-9
- *Steam Locomotives of the B&O Railroad Photo Archive* ISBN 1-58388-095-X
- *Streamliners to the Twin Cities Photo Archive 400, Twin Zephyrs & Hiawatha Trains* ISBN 1-58388-096-8
- *Trains of the Twin Ports Photo Archive, Duluth-Superior in the 1950s* ISBN 1-58388-003-8
- *Trains of the Circus 1872-1956* ISBN 1-58388-024-0
- *Trains of the Upper Midwest Photo Archive Steam & Diesel in the 1950s & 1960s* ISBN 1-58388-036-4
- *Wisconsin Central Limited 1987-1996 Photo Archive* ISBN 1-882256-75-1
- *Wisconsin Central Railway 1871-1909 Photo Archive* ISBN 1-882256-78-6

RECREATIONAL VEHICLES

- *Ski-Doo Racing Sleds 1960-2003 Photo Archive* ISBN 1-58388-105-0

TRUCKS

- *Autocar Trucks 1950-1987 Photo Archive* ISBN 1-58388-072-0
- *Beverage Trucks 1910-1975 Photo Archive* ISBN 1-882256-60-3
- *Brockway Trucks 1948-1961 Photo Archive** ISBN 1-882256-55-7
- *Chevrolet El Camino Photo History Incl. GMC Sprint & Caballero* ISBN 1-58388-044-5
- *Circus and Carnival Trucks 1923-2000 Photo Archive* ISBN 1-58388-048-8
- *Dodge B-Series Trucks Restorer's & Collector's Reference Guide and History* ISBN 1-58388-087-9
- *Dodge Pickups 1939-1978 Photo Album* ISBN 1-882256-82-4
- *Dodge Power Wagons 1940-1980 Photo Archive* ISBN 1-882256-89-1
- *Dodge Power Wagon Photo History* ISBN 1-58388-019-4
- *Dodge Ram Trucks 1994-2001 Photo History* ISBN 1-58388-051-8
- *Dodge Trucks 1929-1947 Photo Archive* ISBN 1-882256-36-0
- *Dodge Trucks 1948-1960 Photo Archive* ISBN 1-882256-37-9
- *Ford 4x4s 1935-1990 Photo History* ISBN 1-58388-079-8
- *Ford Heavy-Duty Trucks 1948-1998 Photo History* ISBN 1-58388-043-7
- *Freightliner Trucks 1937-1981 Photo Archive* ISBN 1-58388-090-9
- *Jeep 1941-2000 Photo Archive* ISBN 1-58388-021-6
- *Jeep Prototypes & Concept Vehicles Photo Archive* ISBN 1-58388-033-X
- *Mack Model AB Photo Archive** ISBN 1-882256-18-2
- *Mack AP Super-Duty Trucks 1926-1938 Photo Archive** ISBN 1-882256-54-9
- *Mack Model B 1953-1966 Volume 2 Photo Archive** ISBN 1-882256-34-4
- *Mack EB-EC-ED-EE-EF-EG-DE 1936-1951 Photo Archive** ISBN 1-882256-29-8
- *Mack EH-EJ-EM-EQ-ER-ES 1936-1950 Photo Archive** ISBN 1-882256-39-5
- *Mack FC-FCSW-NW 1936-1947 Photo Archive** ISBN 1-882256-28-X
- *Mack FG-FH-FJ-FK-FN-FP-FT-FW 1937-1950 Photo Archive** ISBN 1-882256-35-2
- *Mack LF-LH-LJ-LM-LT 1940-1956 Photo Archive** ISBN 1-882256-38-7
- *Mack Trucks Photo Gallery** ISBN 1-882256-88-3
- *New Car Carriers 1910-1998 Photo Album* ISBN 1-882256-98-0
- *Plymouth Commercial Vehicles Photo Archive* ISBN 1-58388-004-6
- *Refuse Trucks Photo Archive* ISBN 1-58388-042-9
- *RVs & Campers 1900-2000: An Illustrated History* ISBN 1-58388-064-X
- *Studebaker Trucks 1927-1940 Photo Archive* ISBN 1-882256-40-9
- *White Trucks 1900-1937 Photo Archive* ISBN 1-882256-80-8

TRACTORS & CONSTRUCTION EQUIPMENT

- *Case Tractors 1912-1959 Photo Archive* ISBN 1-882256-32-8
- *Caterpillar Photo Gallery* ISBN 1-882256-70-0
- *Caterpillar Pocket Guide The Track-Type Tractors 1925-1957* ISBN 1-58388-022-4
- *Caterpillar D-2 & R-2 Photo Archive* ISBN 1-882256-99-9
- *Caterpillar D-8 1933-1974 Photo Archive Incl. Diesel 75 & RD-8* ISBN 1-882256-96-4
- *Caterpillar Military Tractors Volume 1 Photo Archive* ISBN 1-882256-16-6
- *Caterpillar Military Tractors Volume 2 Photo Archive* ISBN 1-882256-17-4
- *Caterpillar Sixty Photo Archive* ISBN 1-882256-05-0
- *Caterpillar Ten Photo Archive Incl. 7c Fifteen & High Fifteen* ISBN 1-58388-011-9
- *Caterpillar Thirty Photo Archive 2ND Ed. Incl. Best Thirty, 6G Thirty & R-4* ISBN 1-58388-006-2
- *Circus & Carnival Tractors 1930-2001 Photo Archive* ISBN 1-58388-076-3
- *Cletrac and Oliver Crawlers Photo Archive* ISBN 1-882256-43-3
- *Classic American Steamrollers 1871-1935 Photo Archive* ISBN 1-58388-038-0
- *Farmall Cub Photo Archive* ISBN 1-882256-71-9
- *Farmall F–Series Photo Archive* ISBN 1-882256-02-6
- *Farmall Model H Photo Archive* ISBN 1-882256-03-4
- *Farmall Model M Photo Archive* ISBN 1-882256-15-8
- *Farmall Regular Photo Archive* ISBN 1-882256-14-X
- *Farmall Super Series Photo Archive* ISBN 1-882256-49-2
- *Fordson 1917-1928 Photo Archive* ISBN 1-882256-33-6
- *Hart-Parr Photo Archive* ISBN 1-882256-08-5
- *Holt Tractors Photo Archive* ISBN 1-882256-10-7
- *International TracTracTor Photo Archive* ISBN 1-882256-48-4
- *John Deere Model A Photo Archive* ISBN 1-882256-12-3
- *John Deere Model D Photo Archive* ISBN 1-882256-00-X
- *Marion Construction Machinery 1884-1975 Photo Archive* ISBN 1-58388-060-7
- *Marion Mining & Dredging Machines Photo Archive* ISBN 1-58388-088-7
- *Oliver Tractors Photo Archive* ISBN 1-882256-09-3
- *Russell Graders Photo Archive* ISBN 1-882256-11-5
- *Twin City Tractor Photo Archive* ISBN 1-882256-06-9